I am deeply grateful to God for all the blessings I have received. I firmly believe that the purpose of life lies in giving meaning to the lives of others. Ronaldh W., Elói K., and Edna C., you are the embodiment of this purpose in my journey. Your presence and support have been the beacon that lights my path, making each step meaningful and each challenge an opportunity for growth. Thank you for being the meaning of my life.

I love you.

Ronaldo Quirino
2024

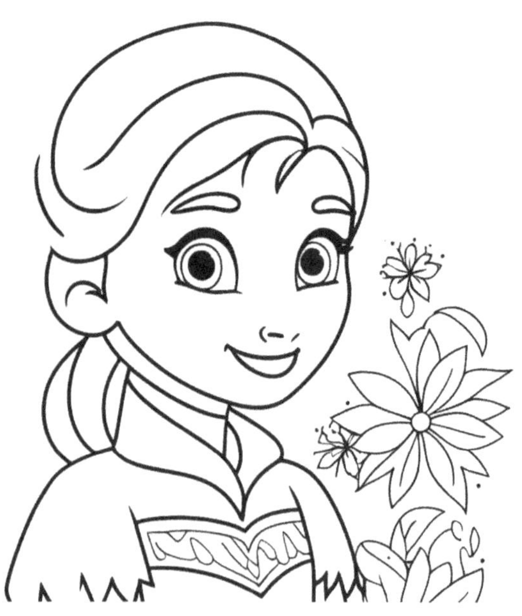
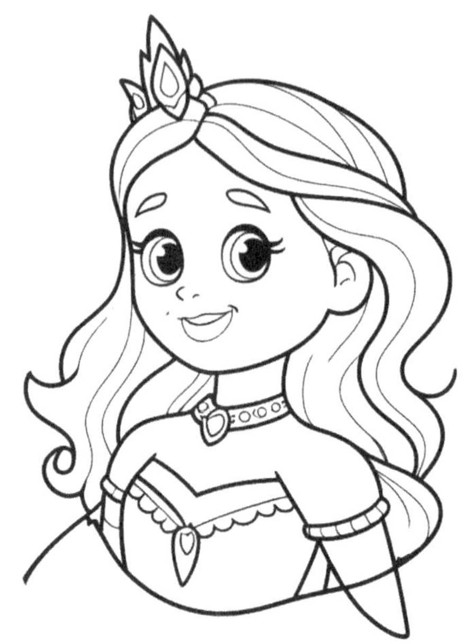

This Book Belongs to:

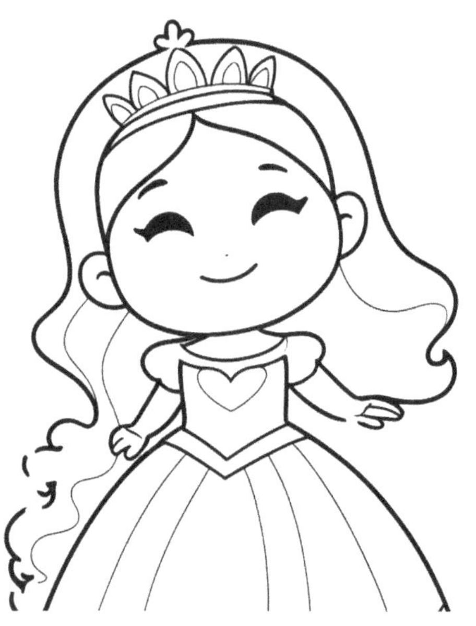
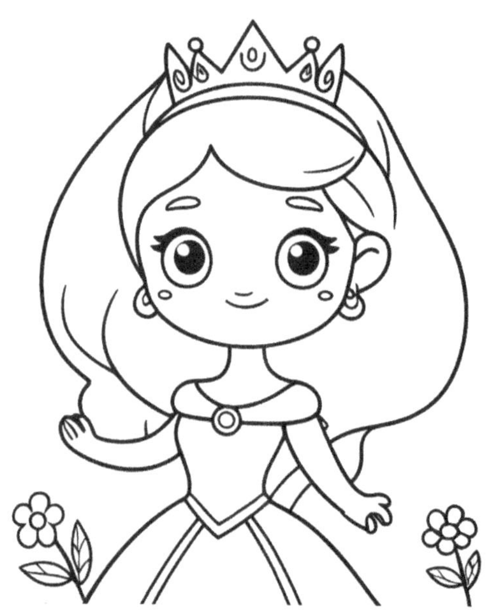

Test Color Page

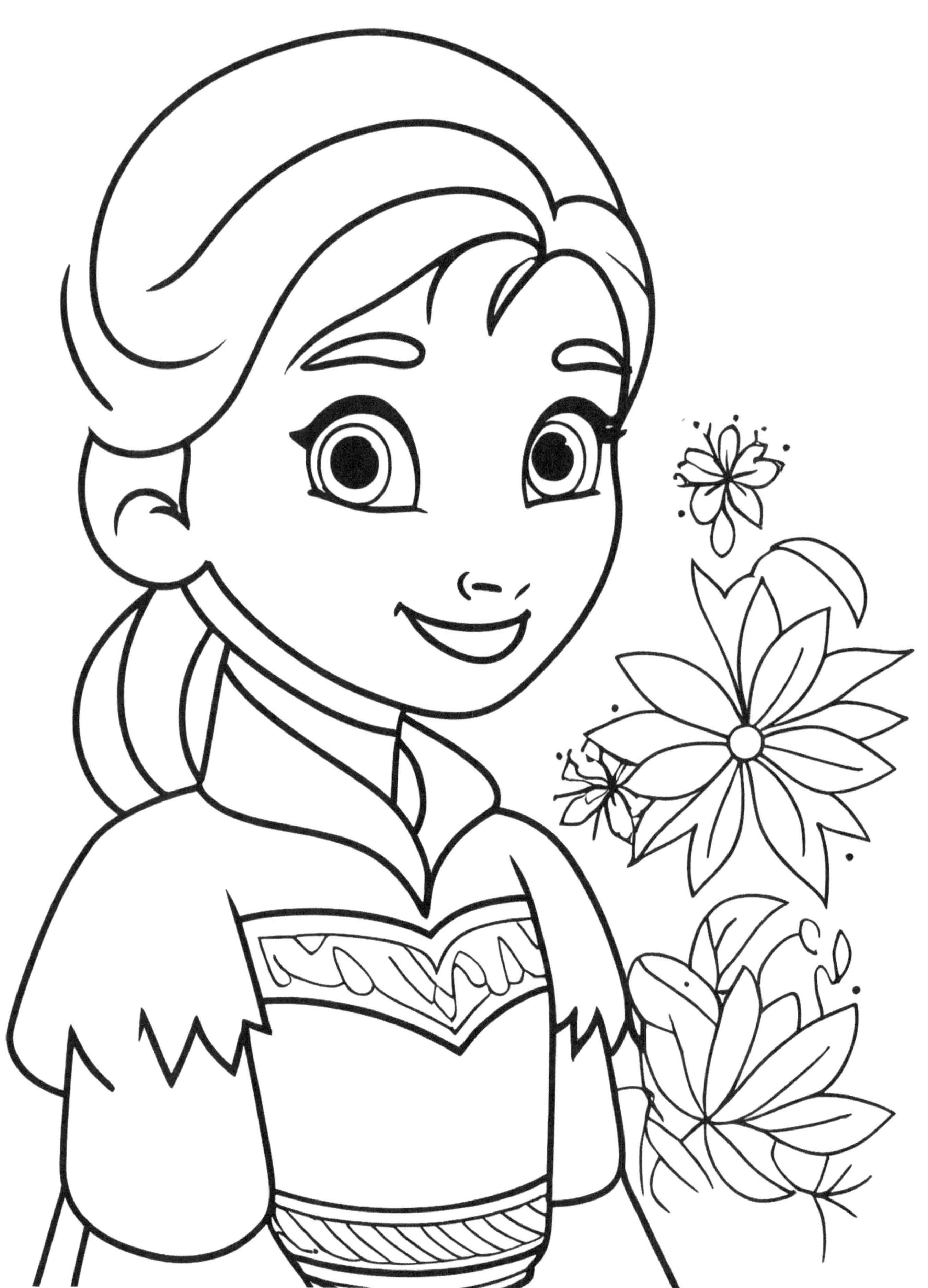

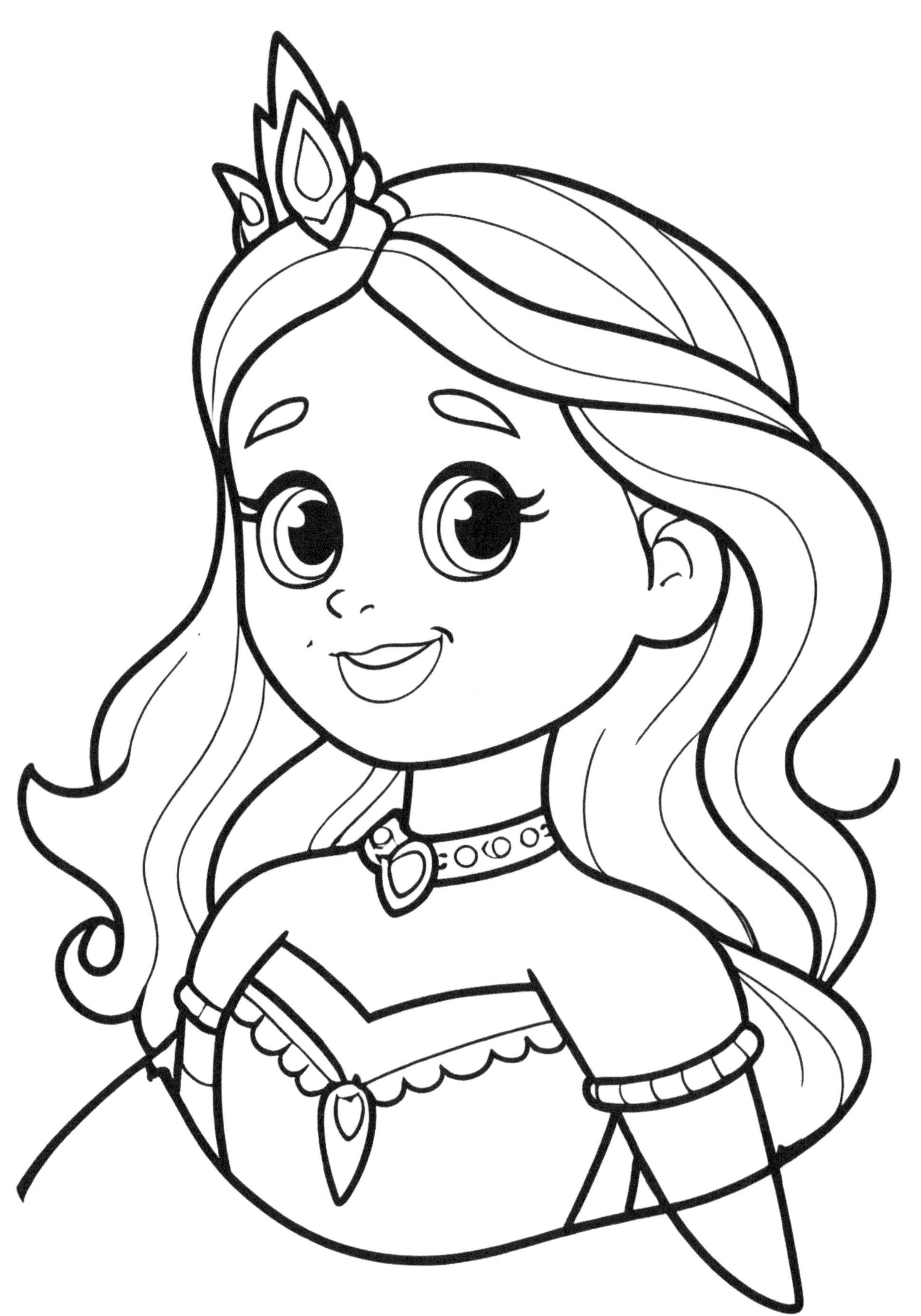

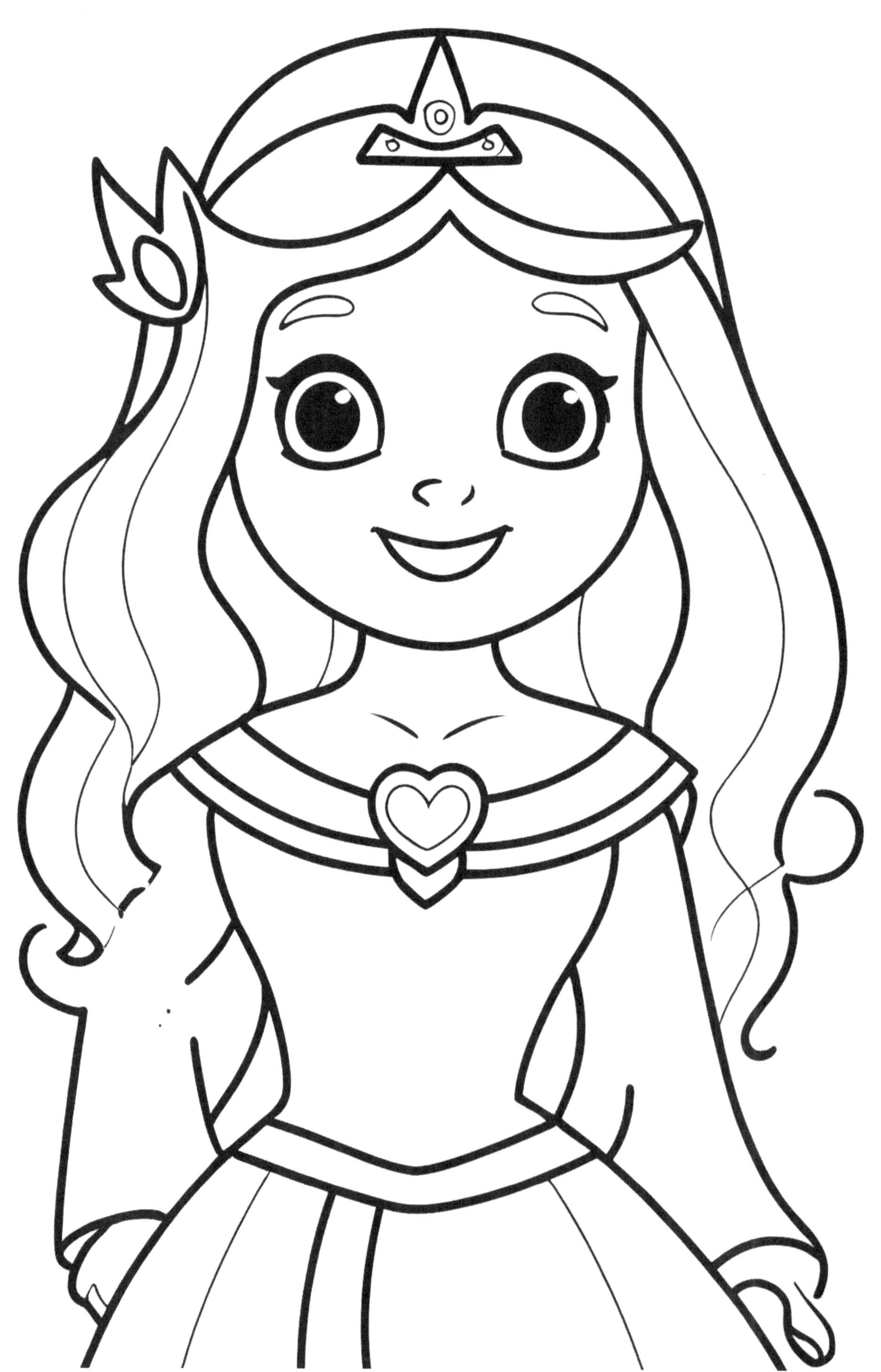

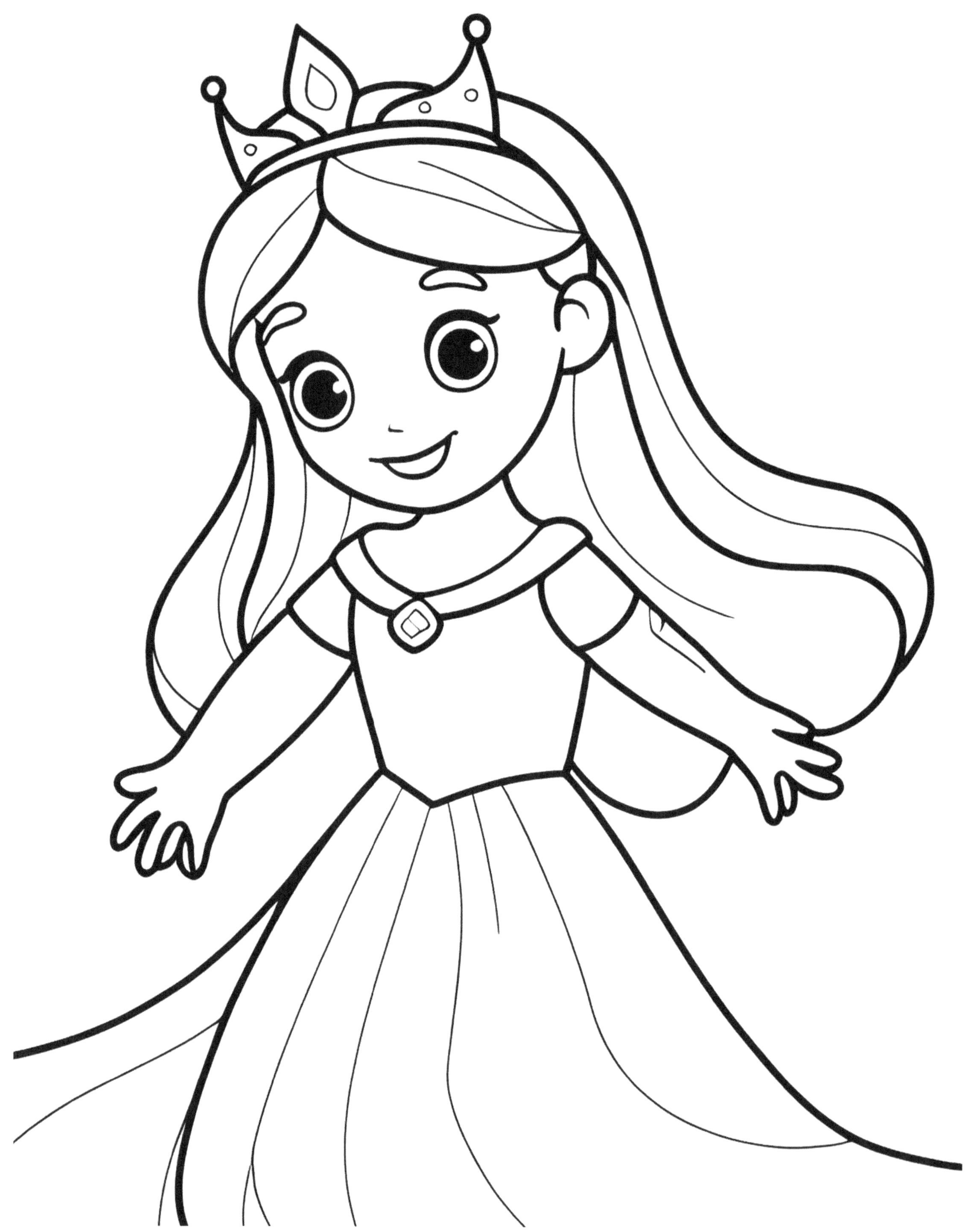

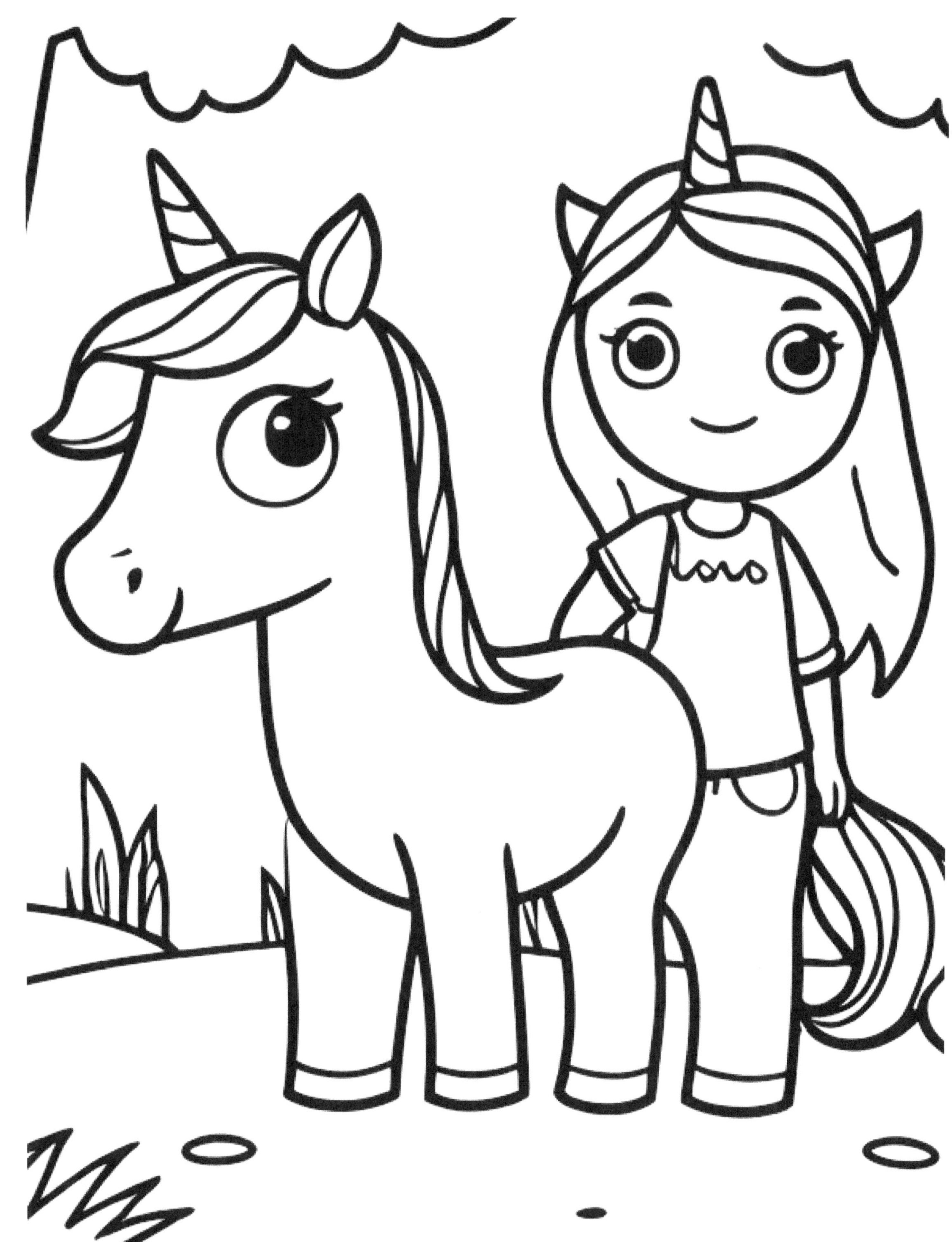

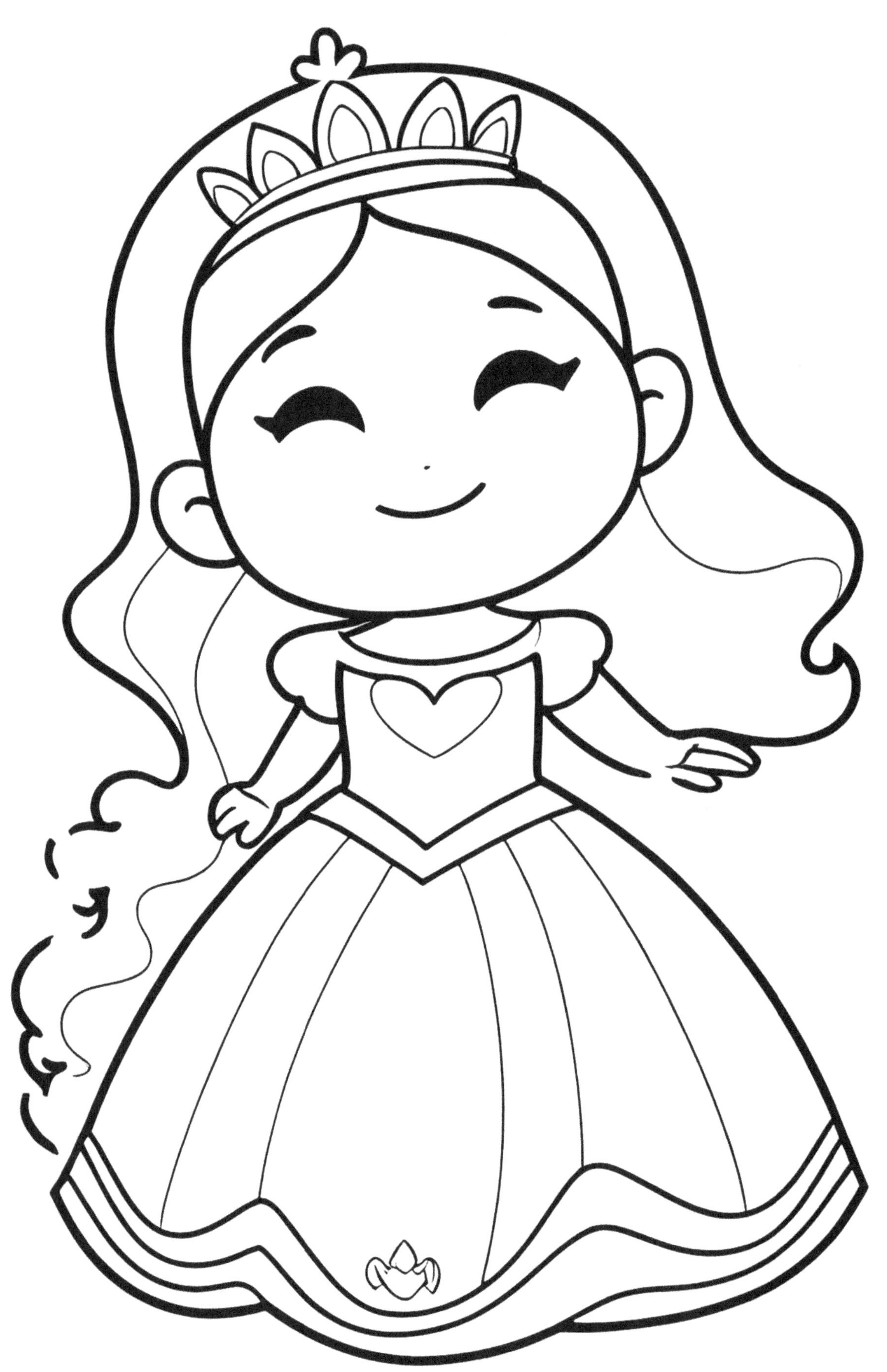

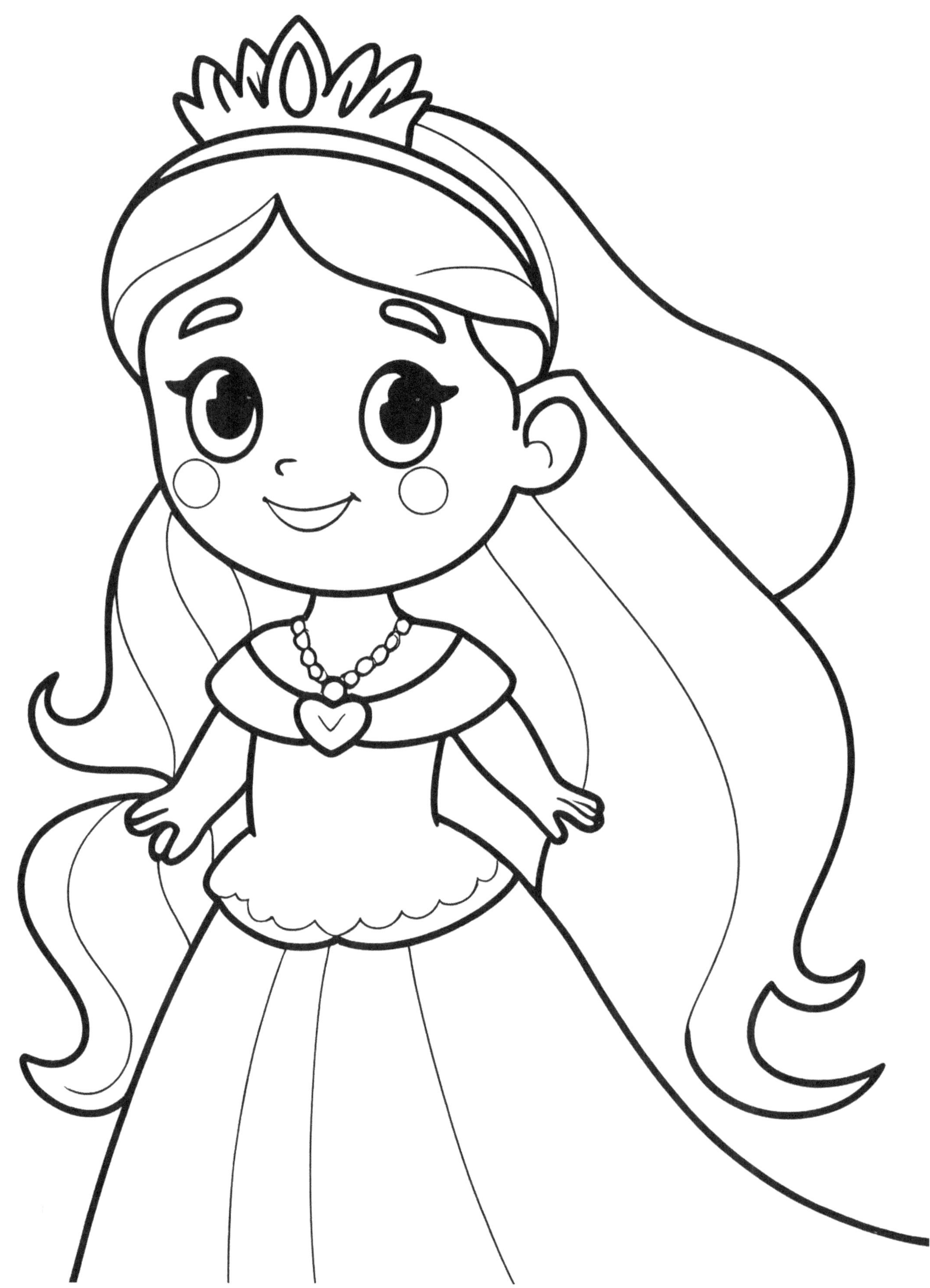

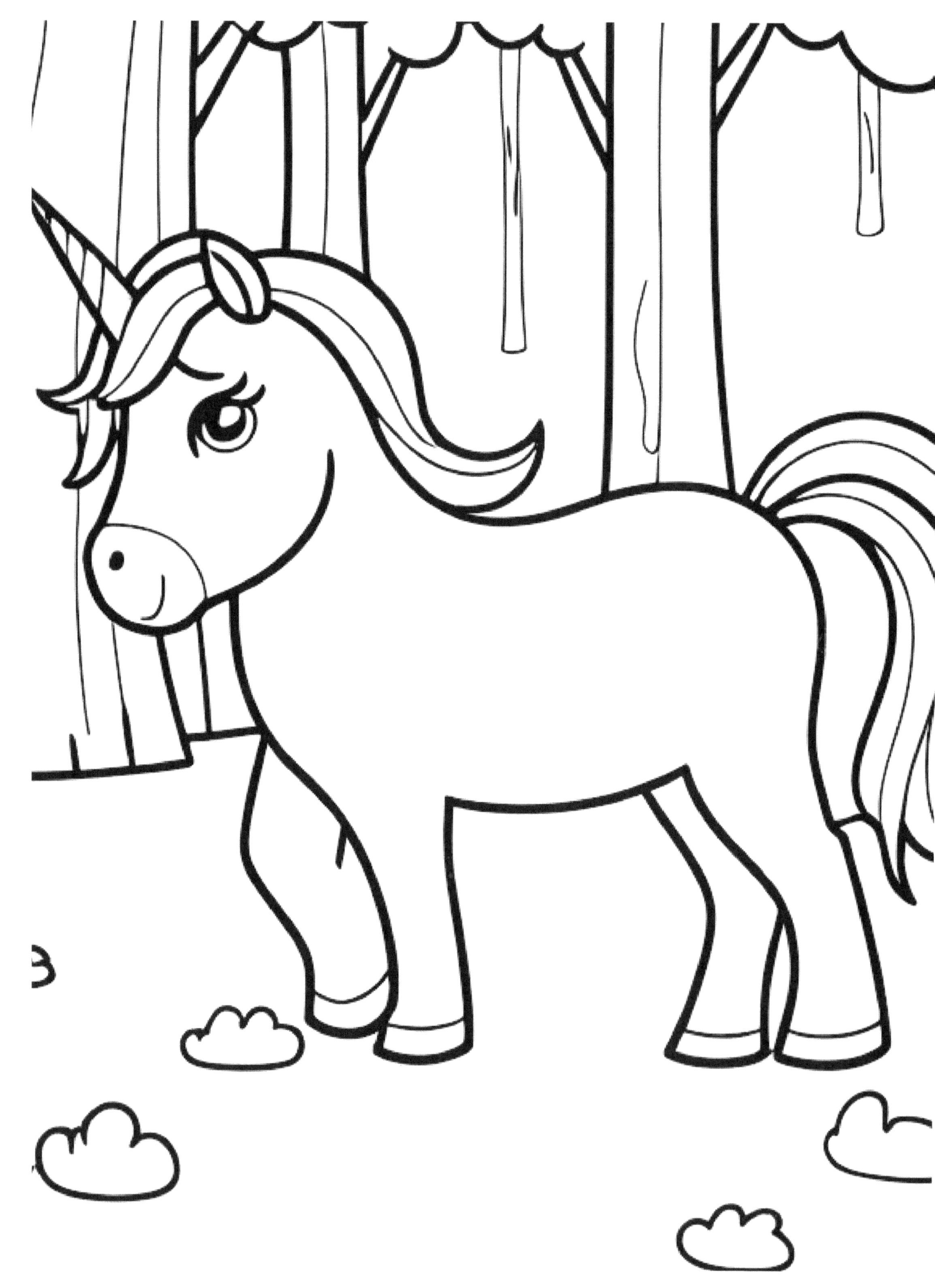

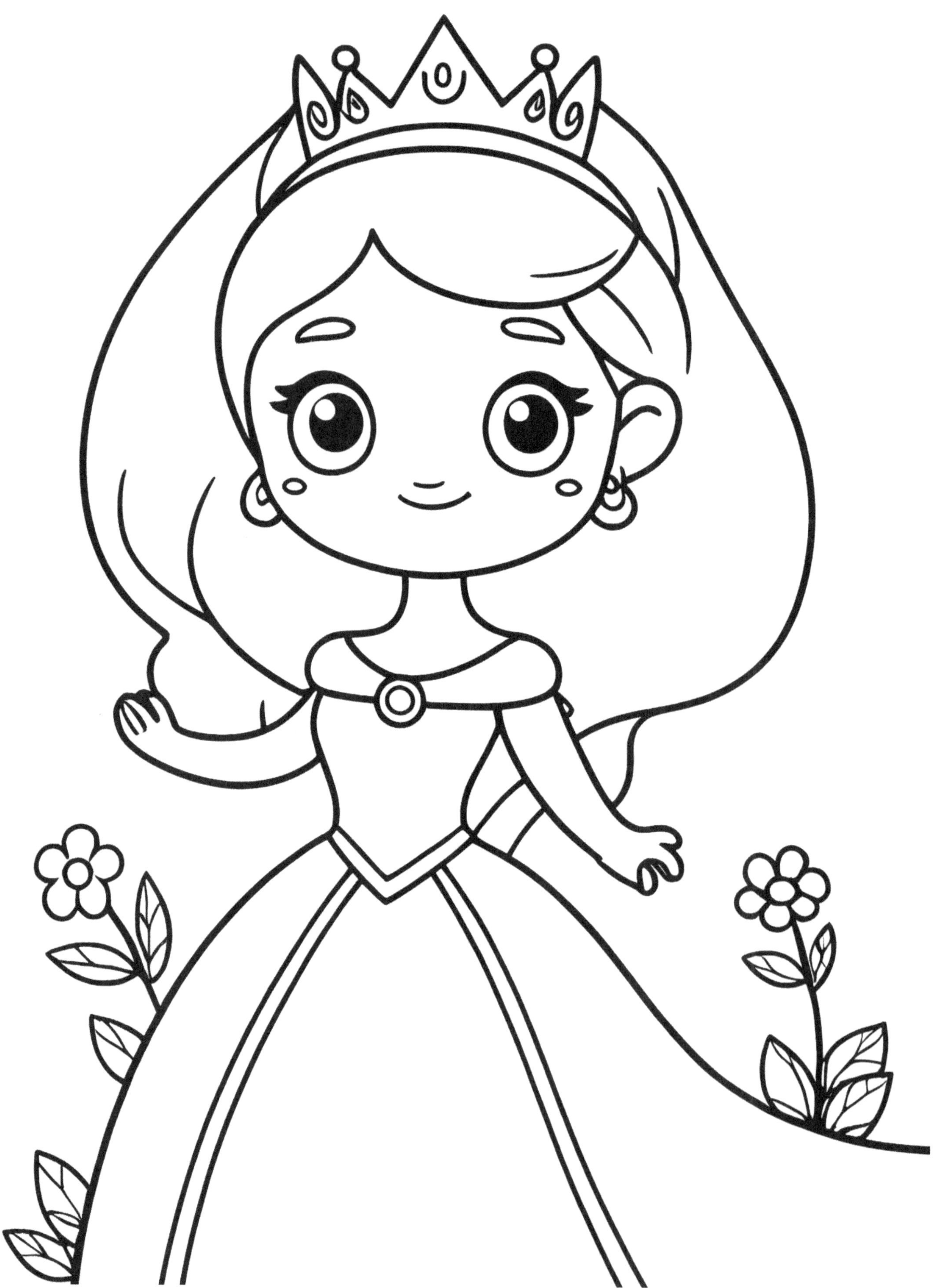

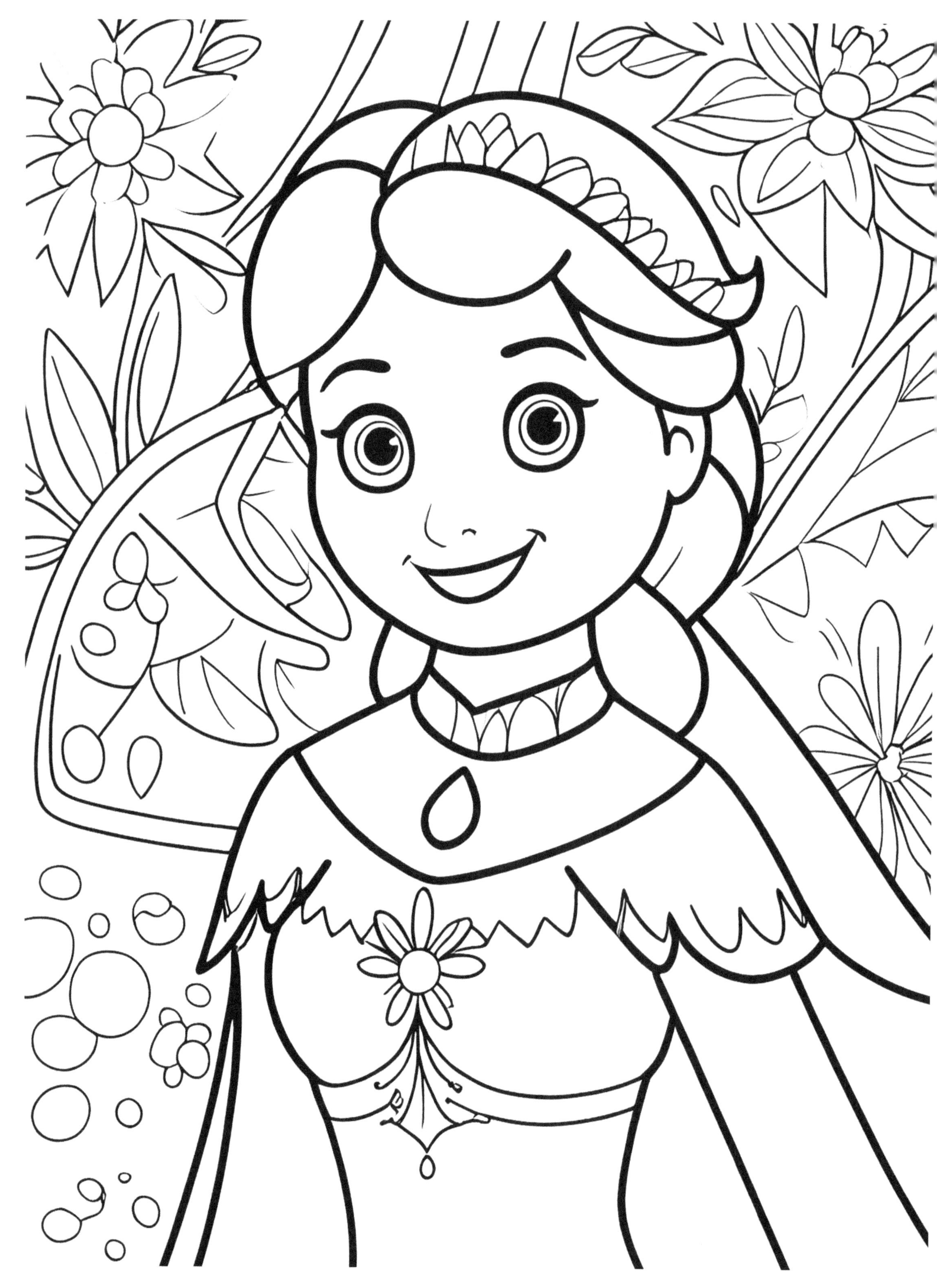

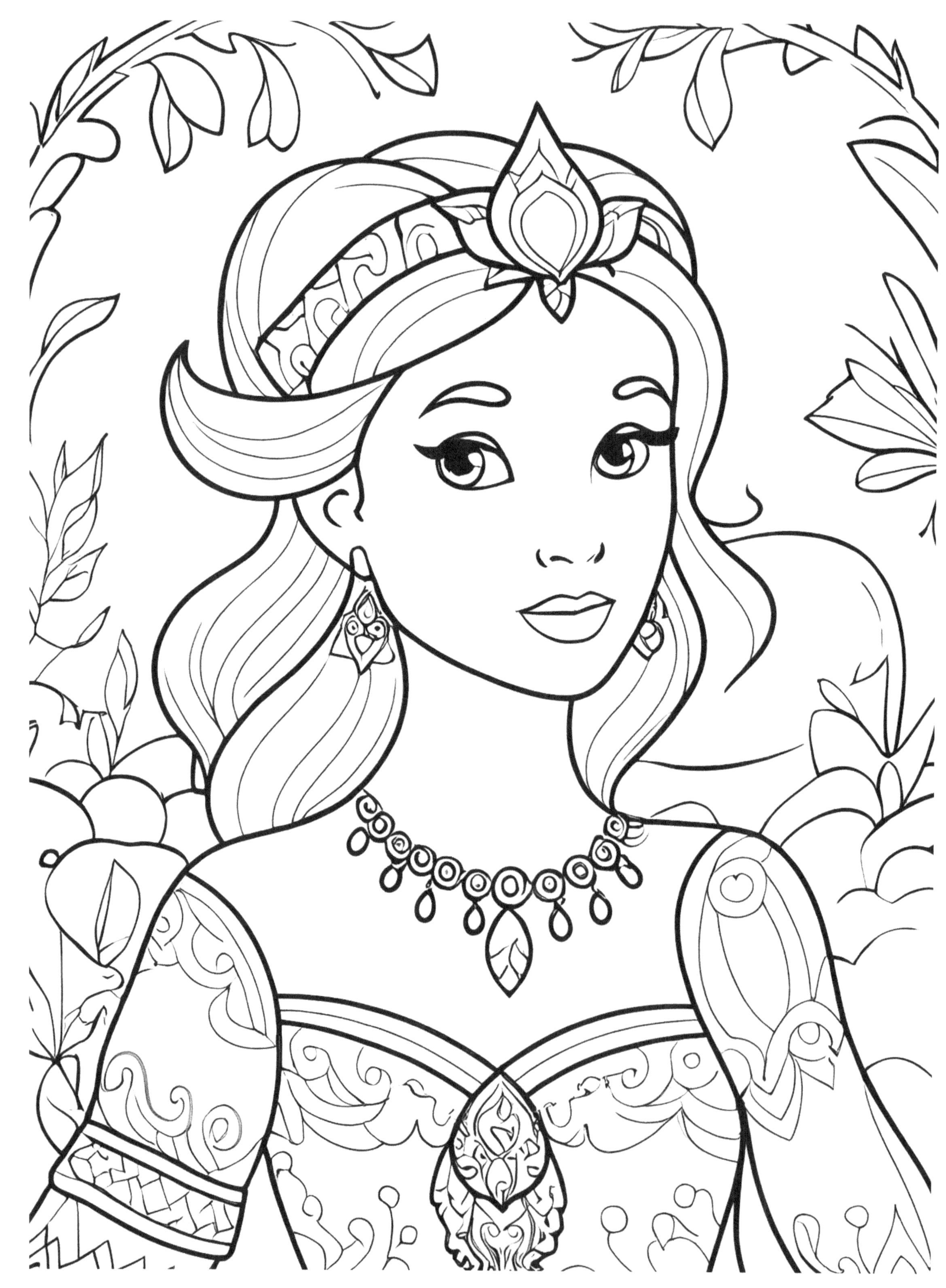

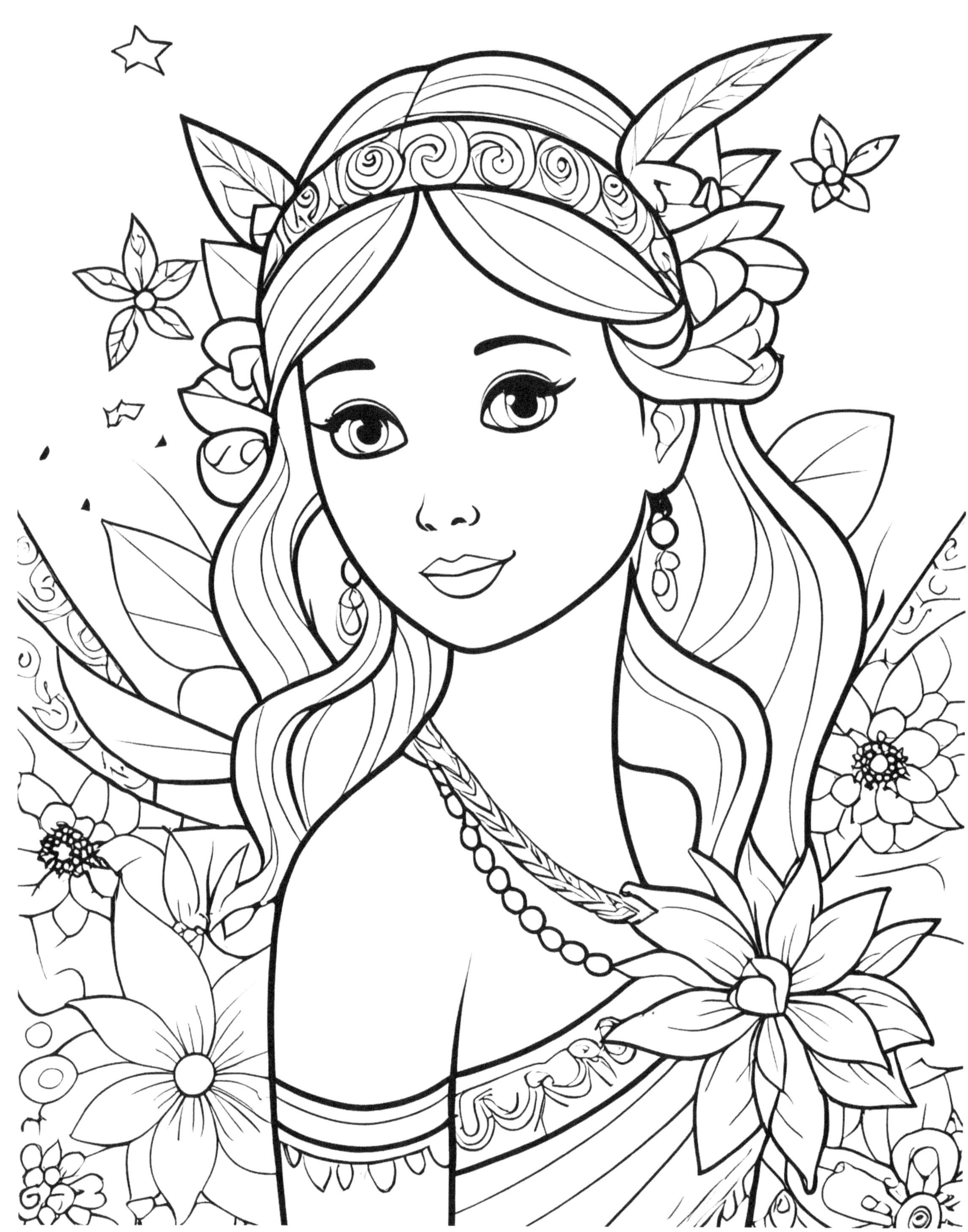

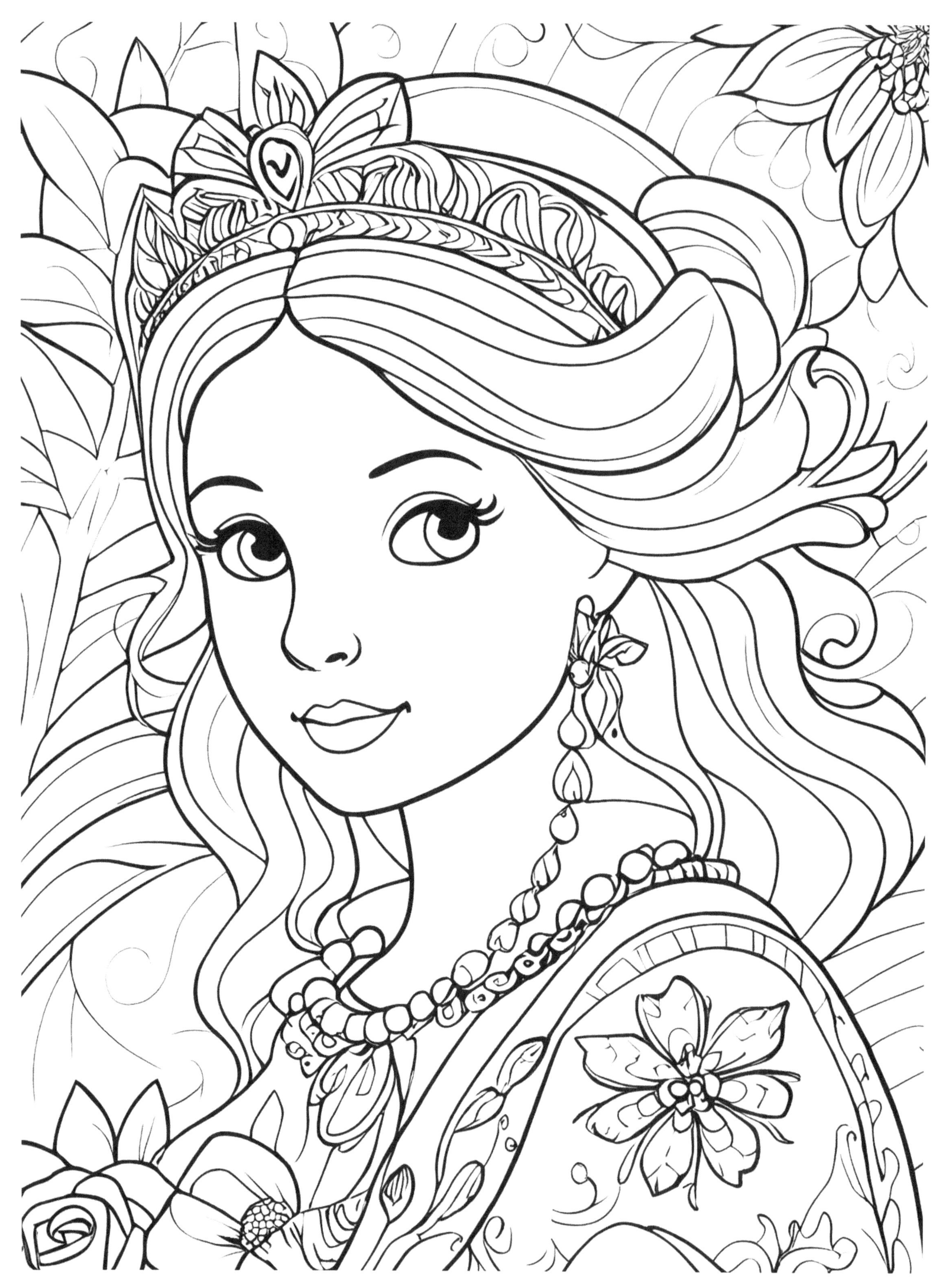

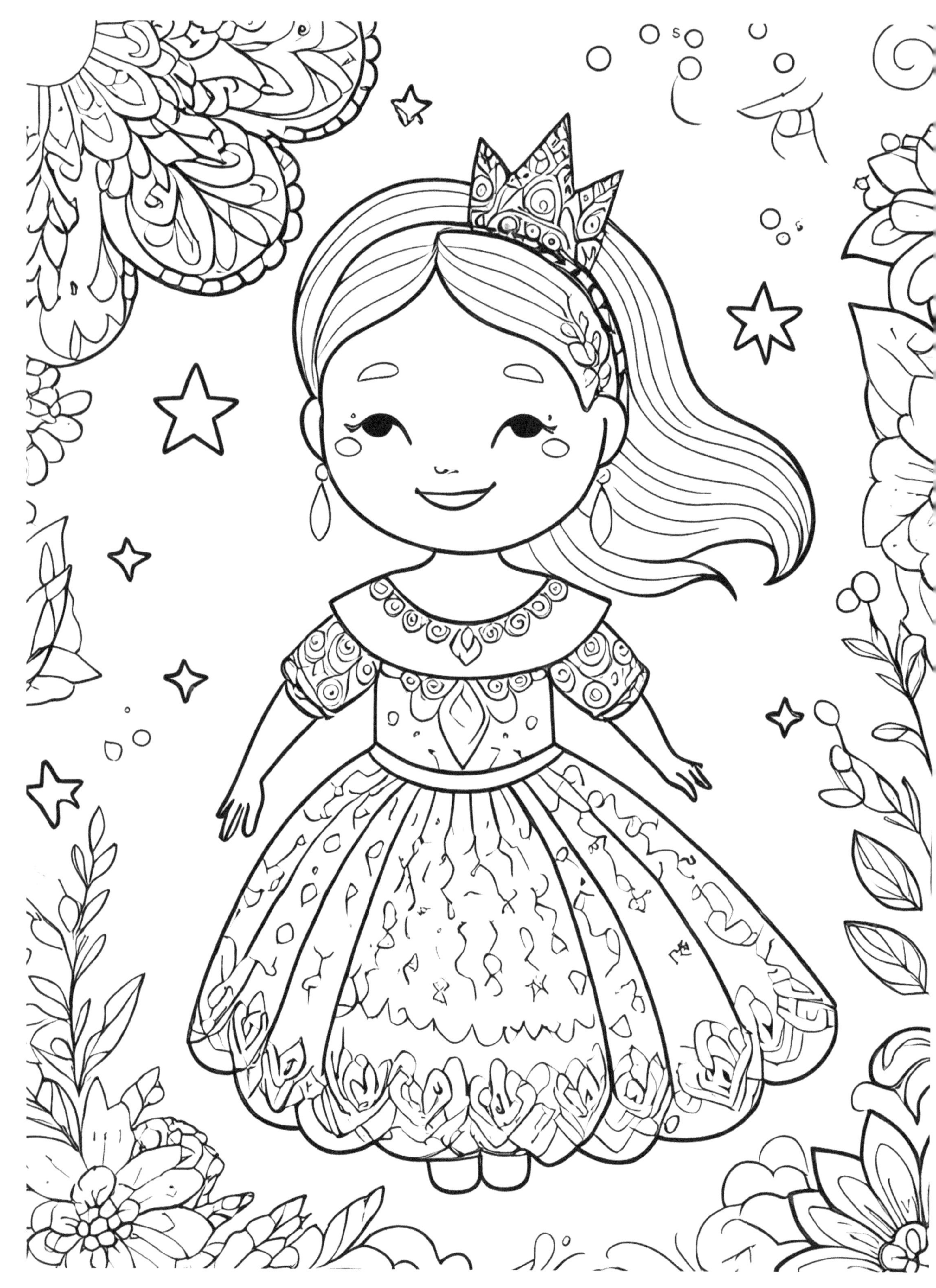

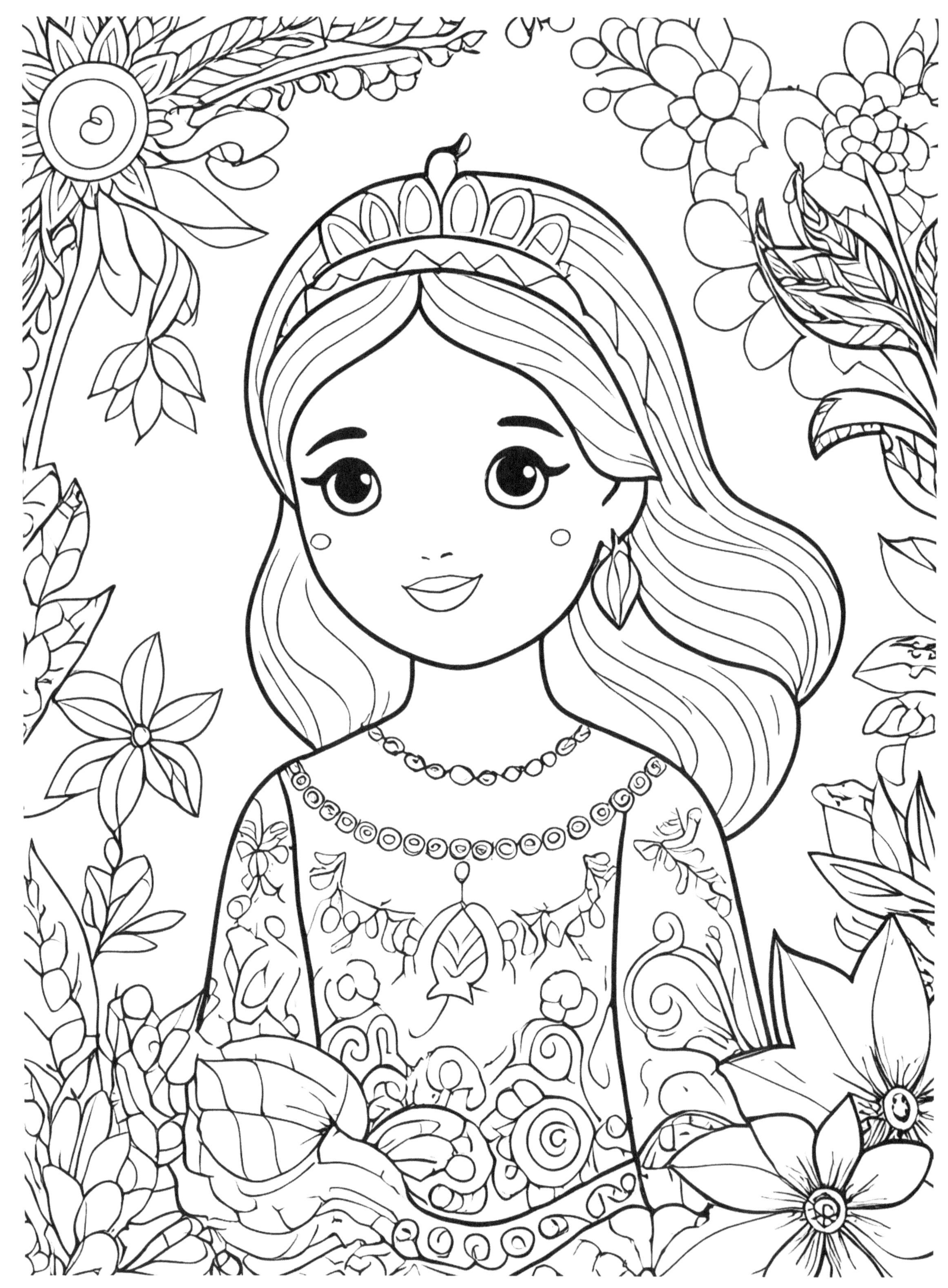

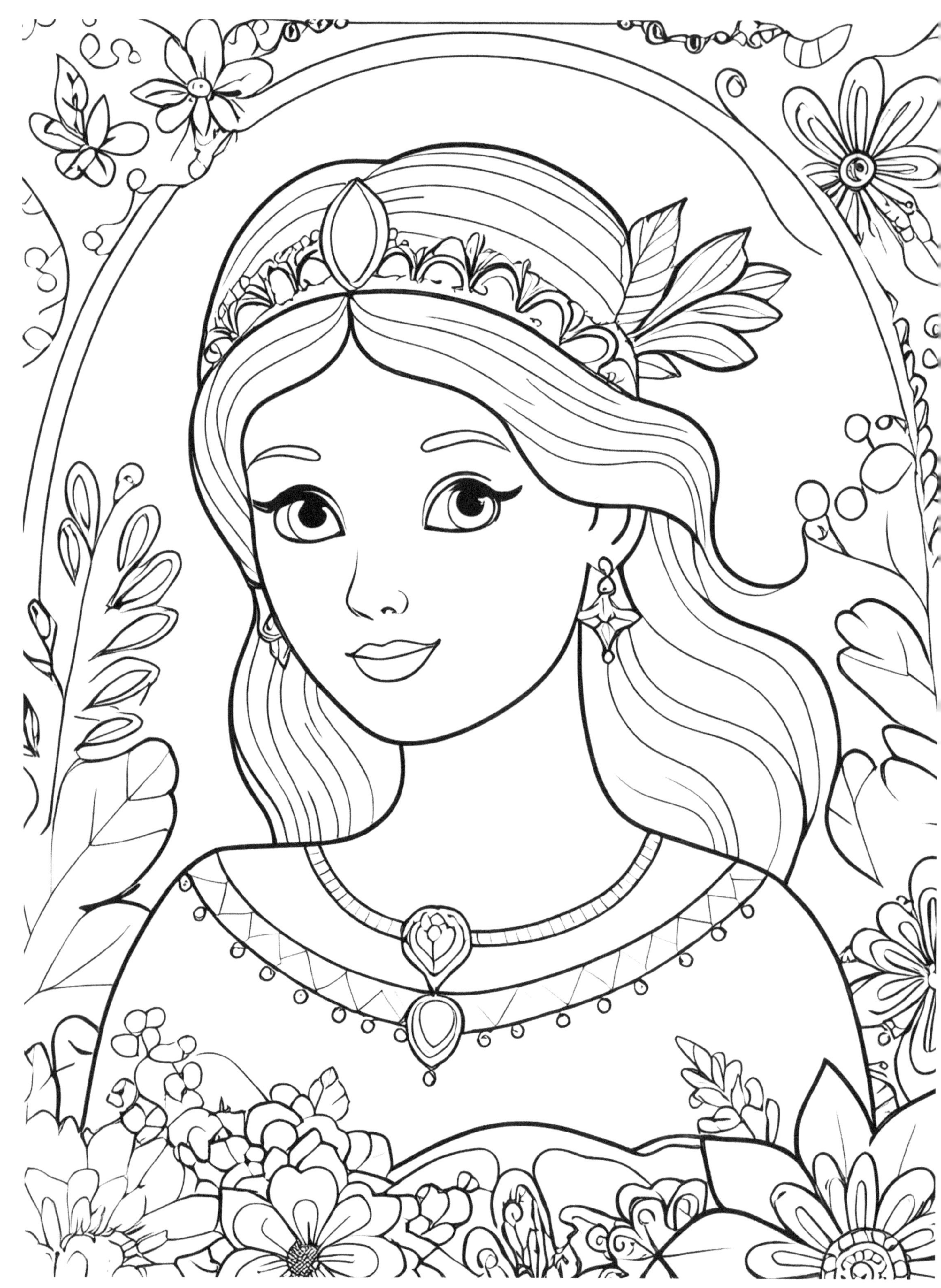

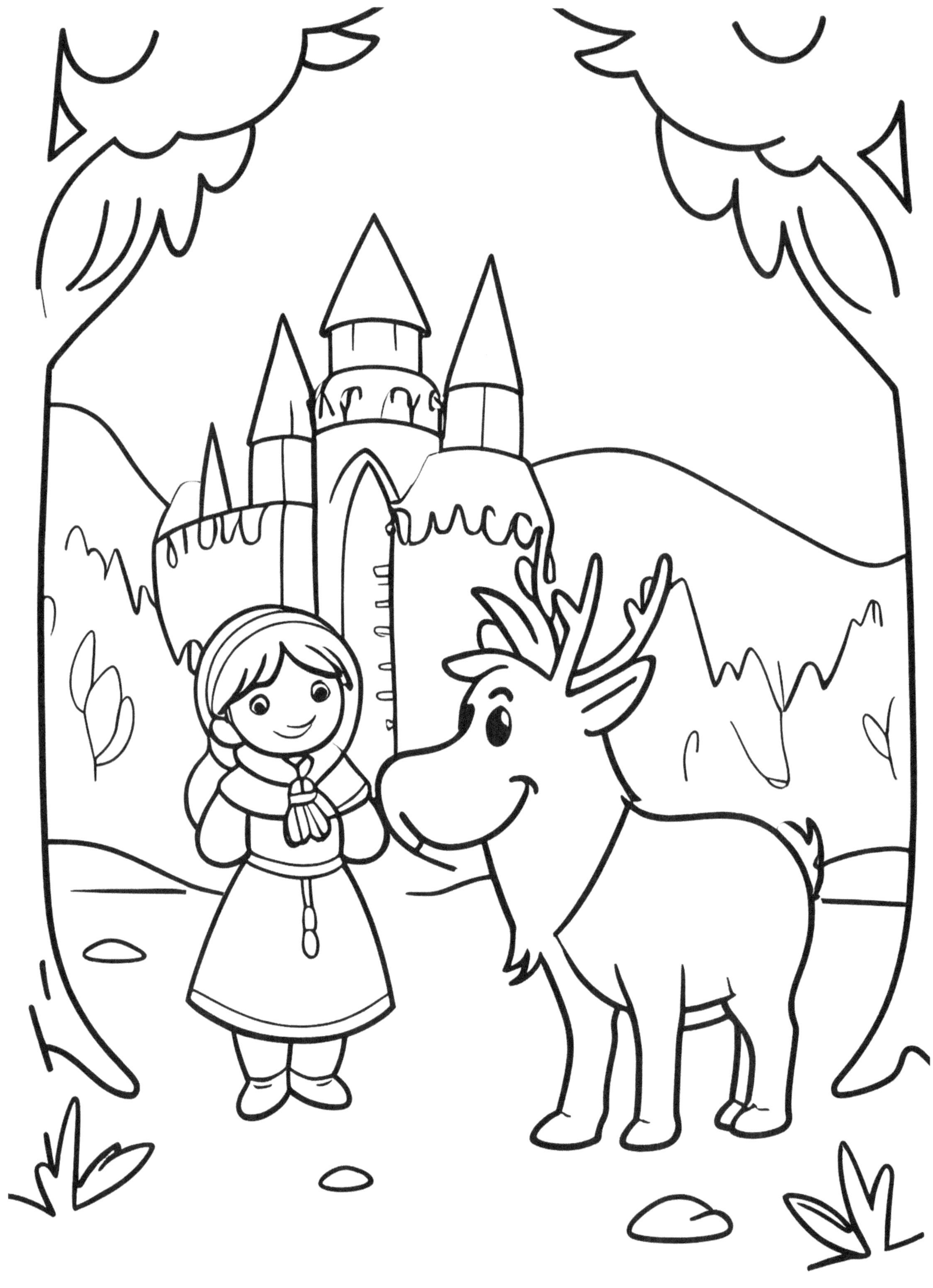

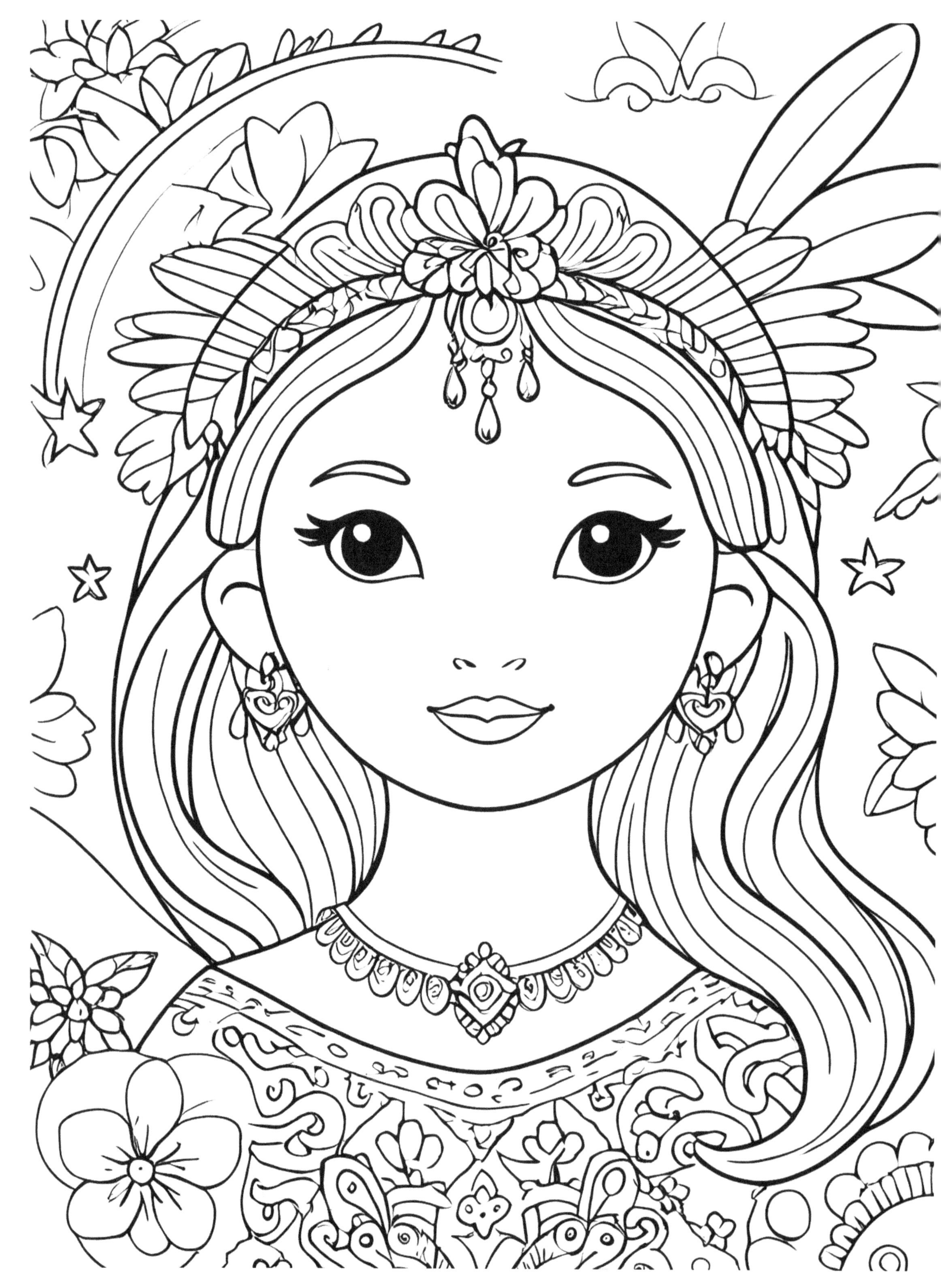

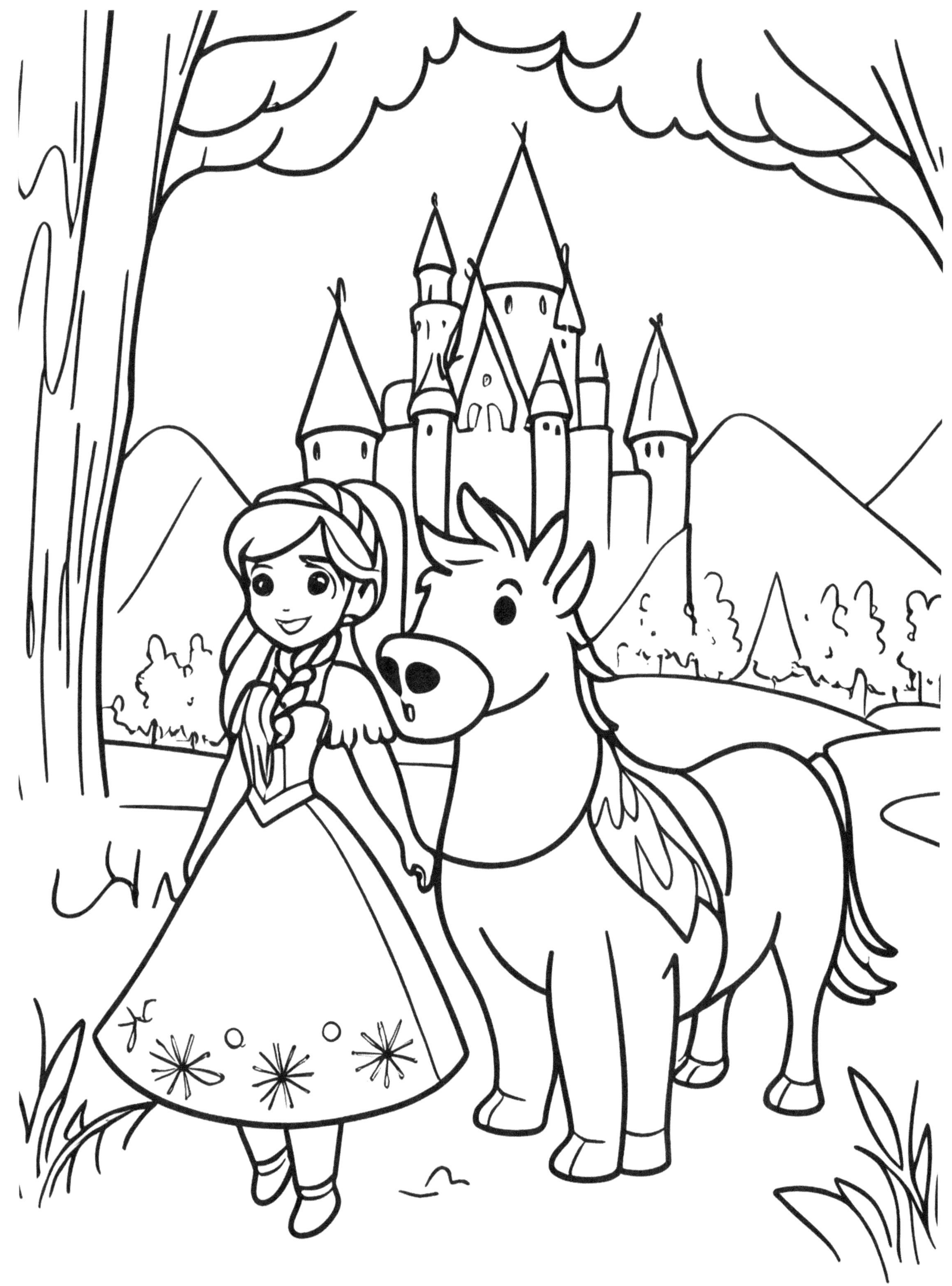

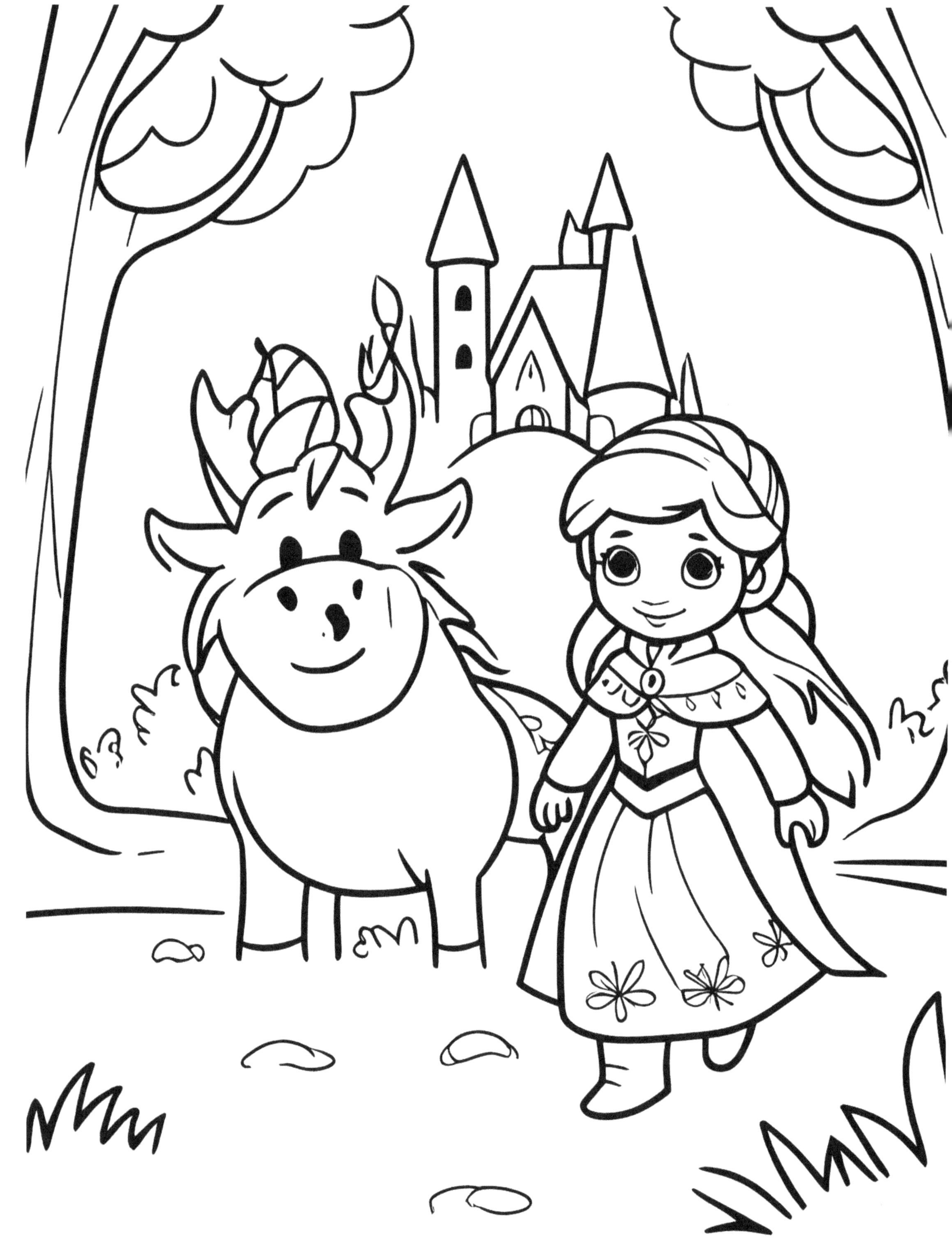

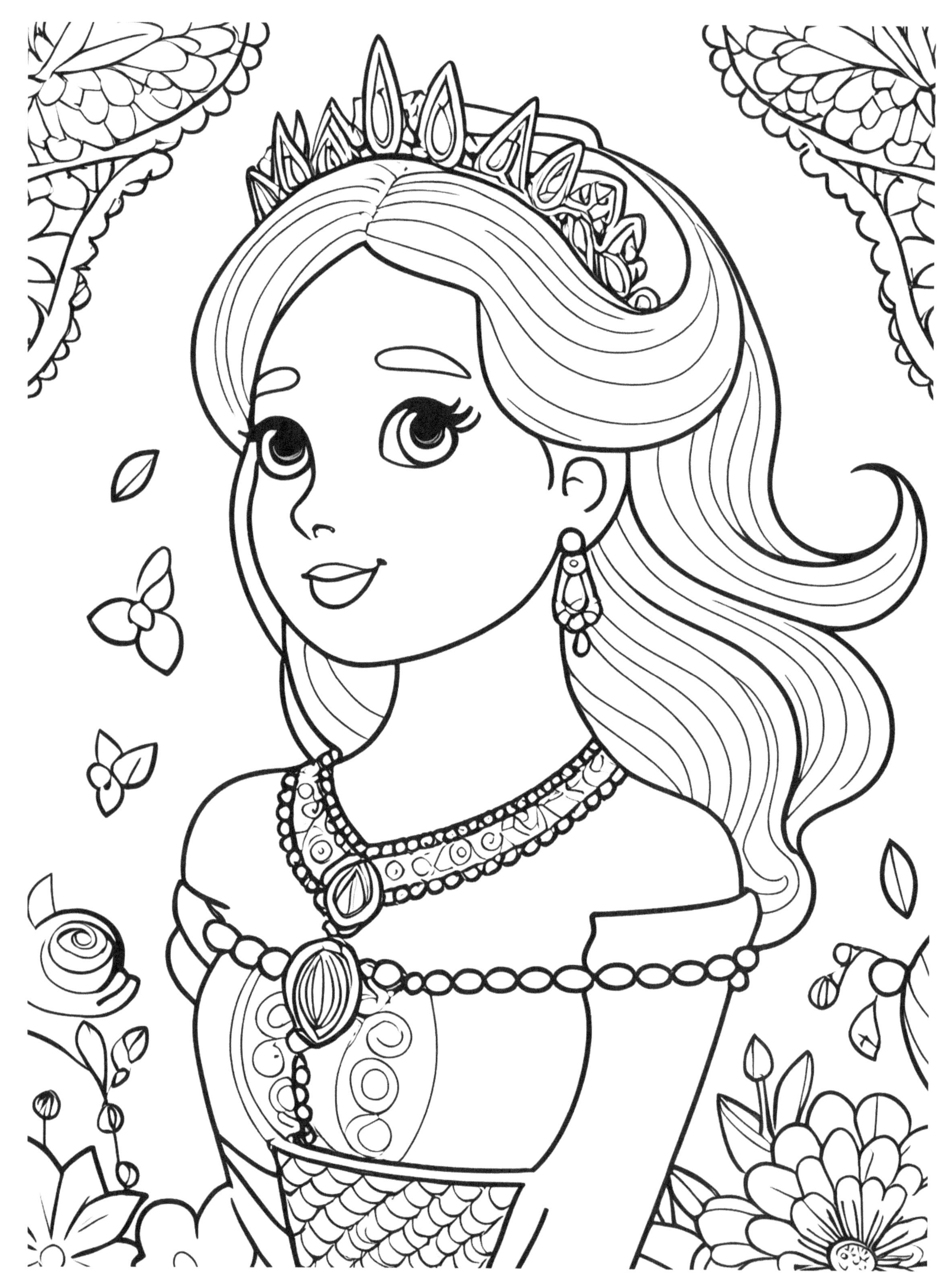

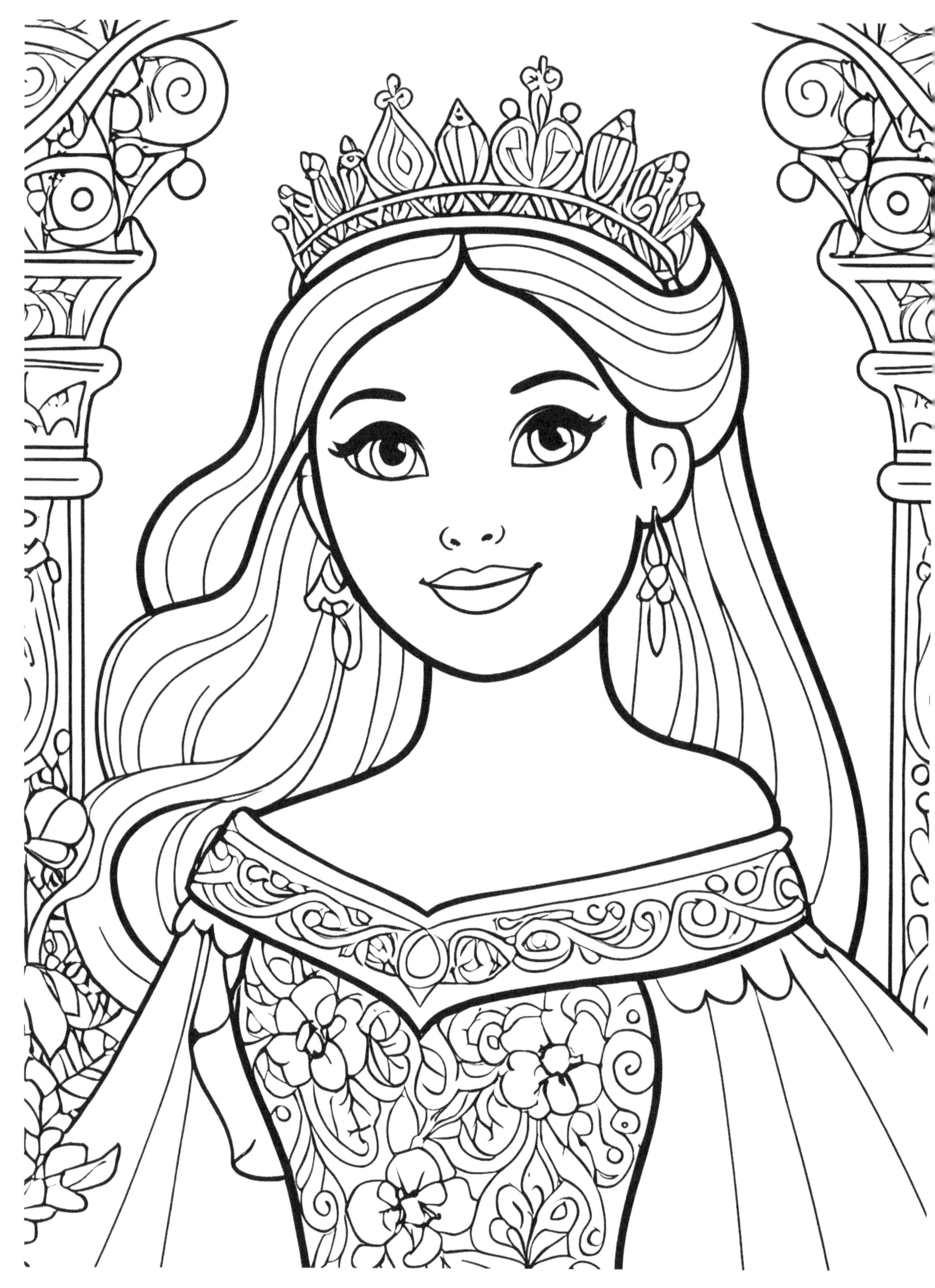

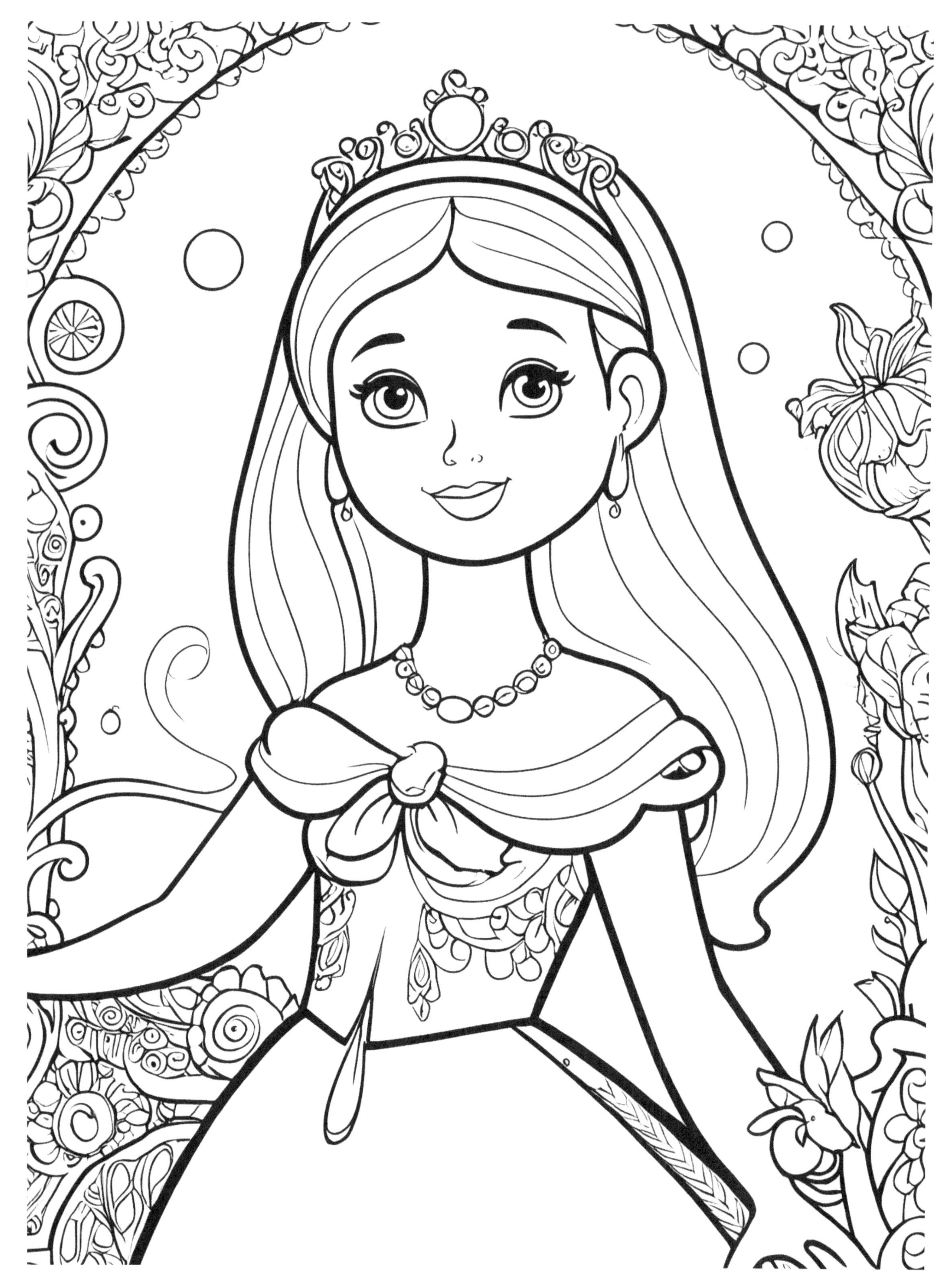

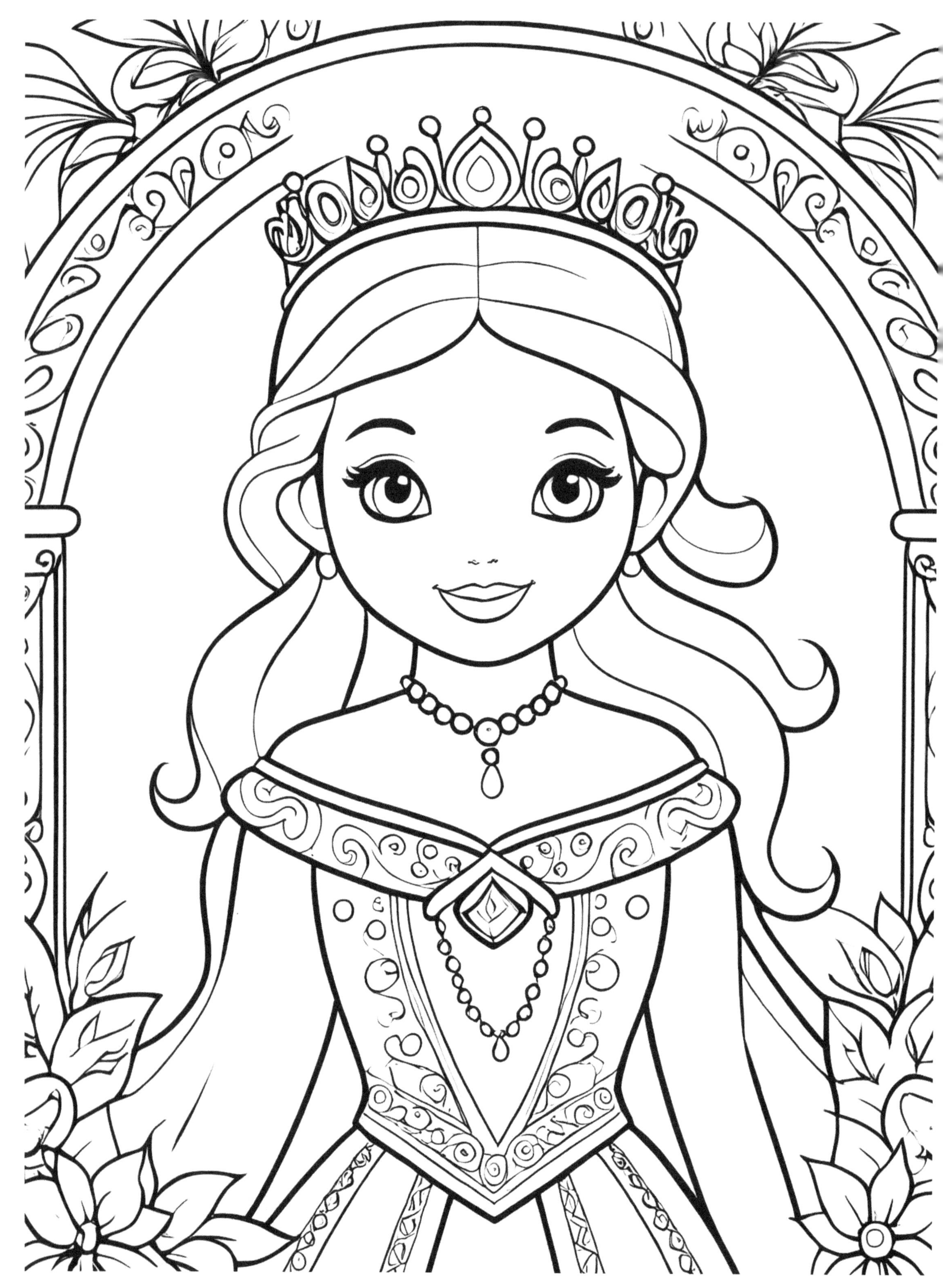

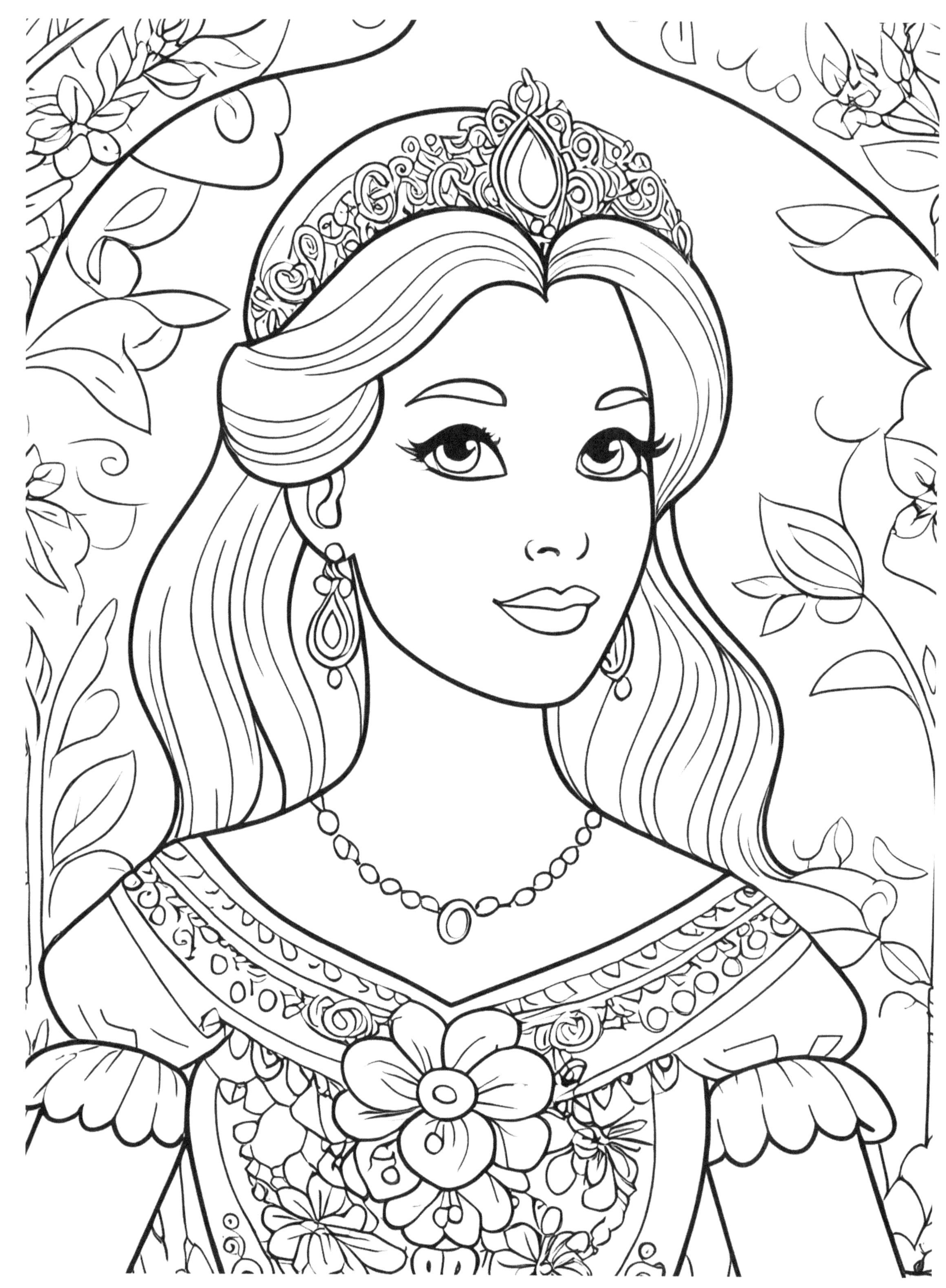

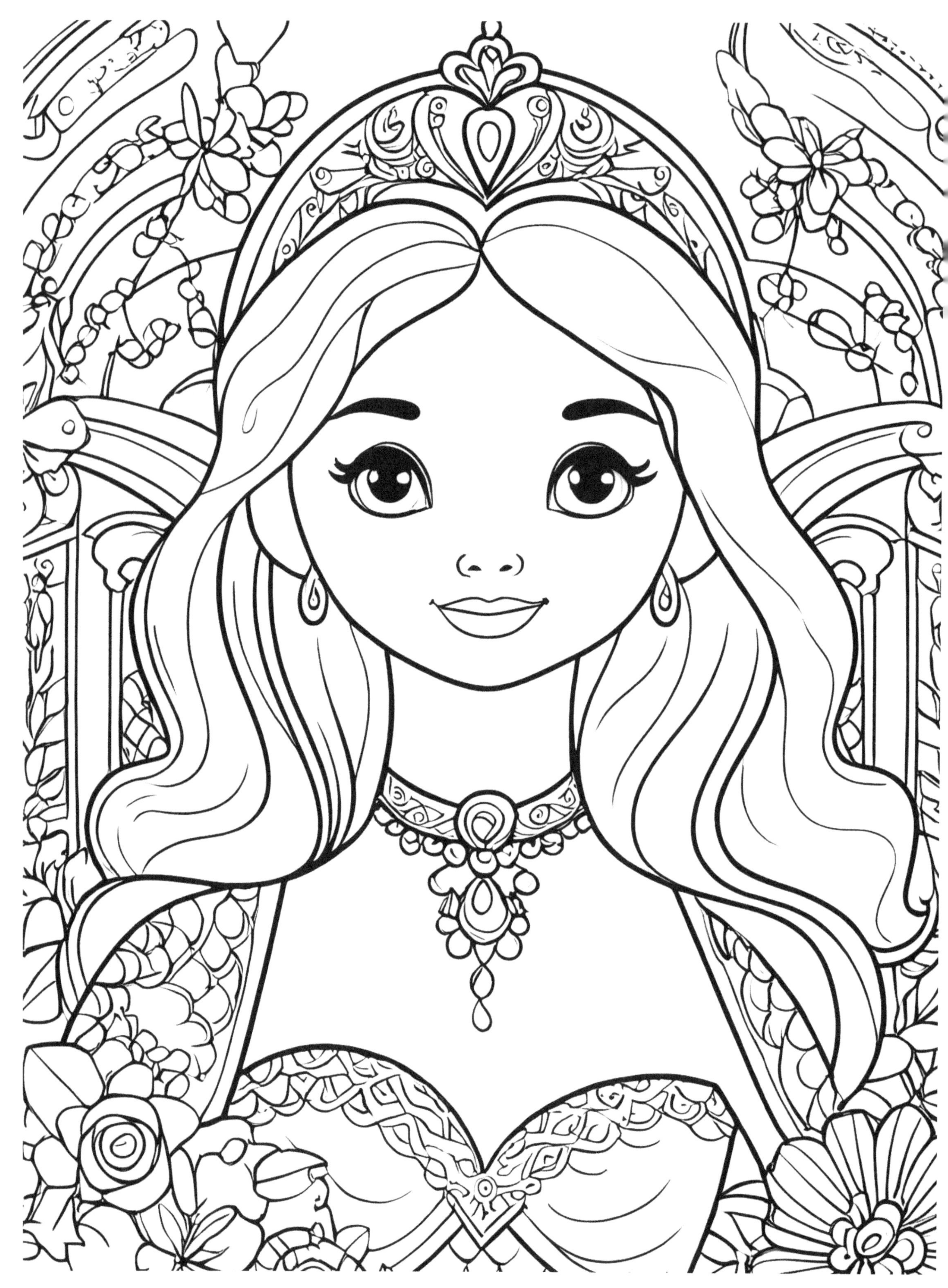

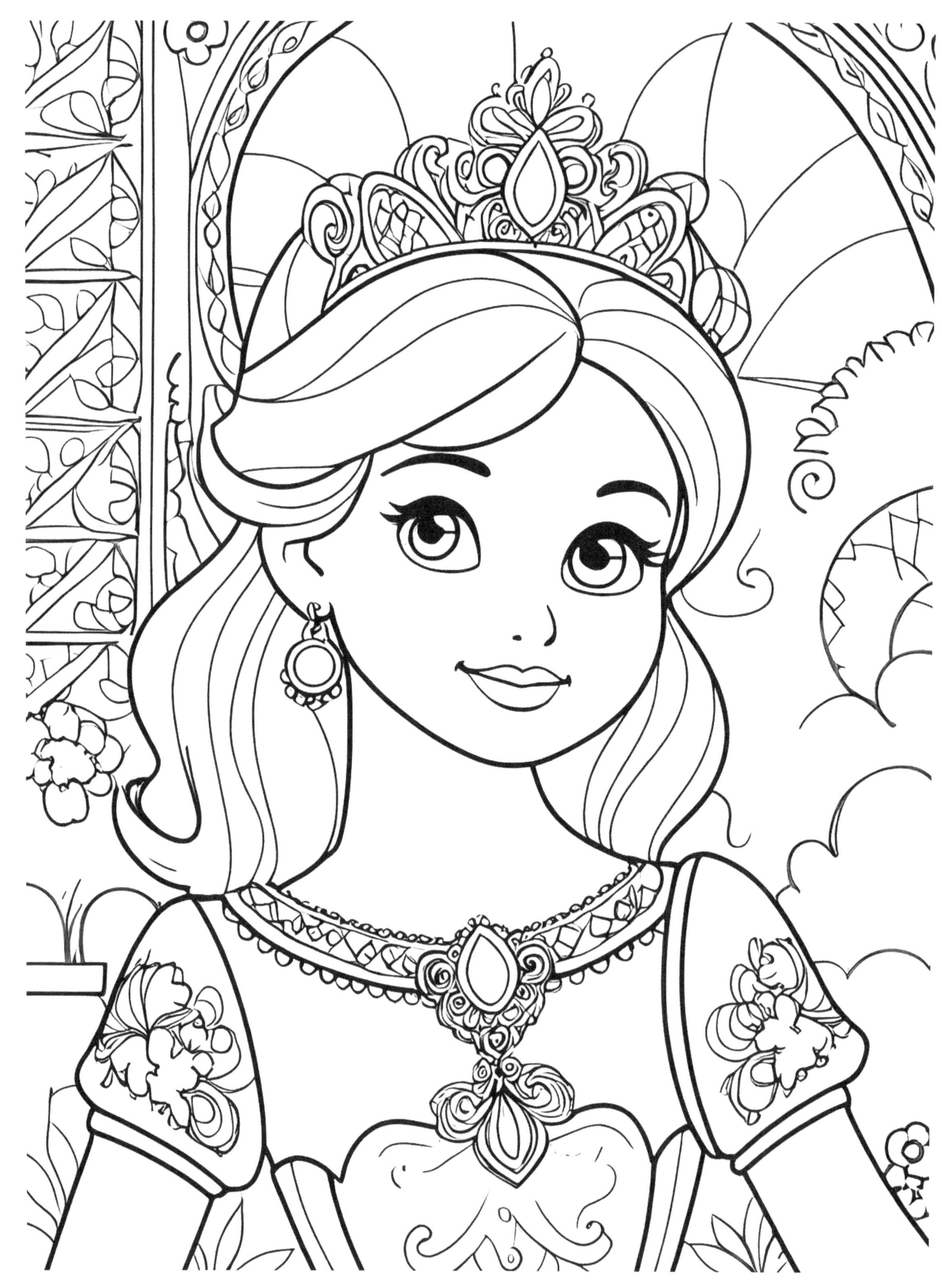

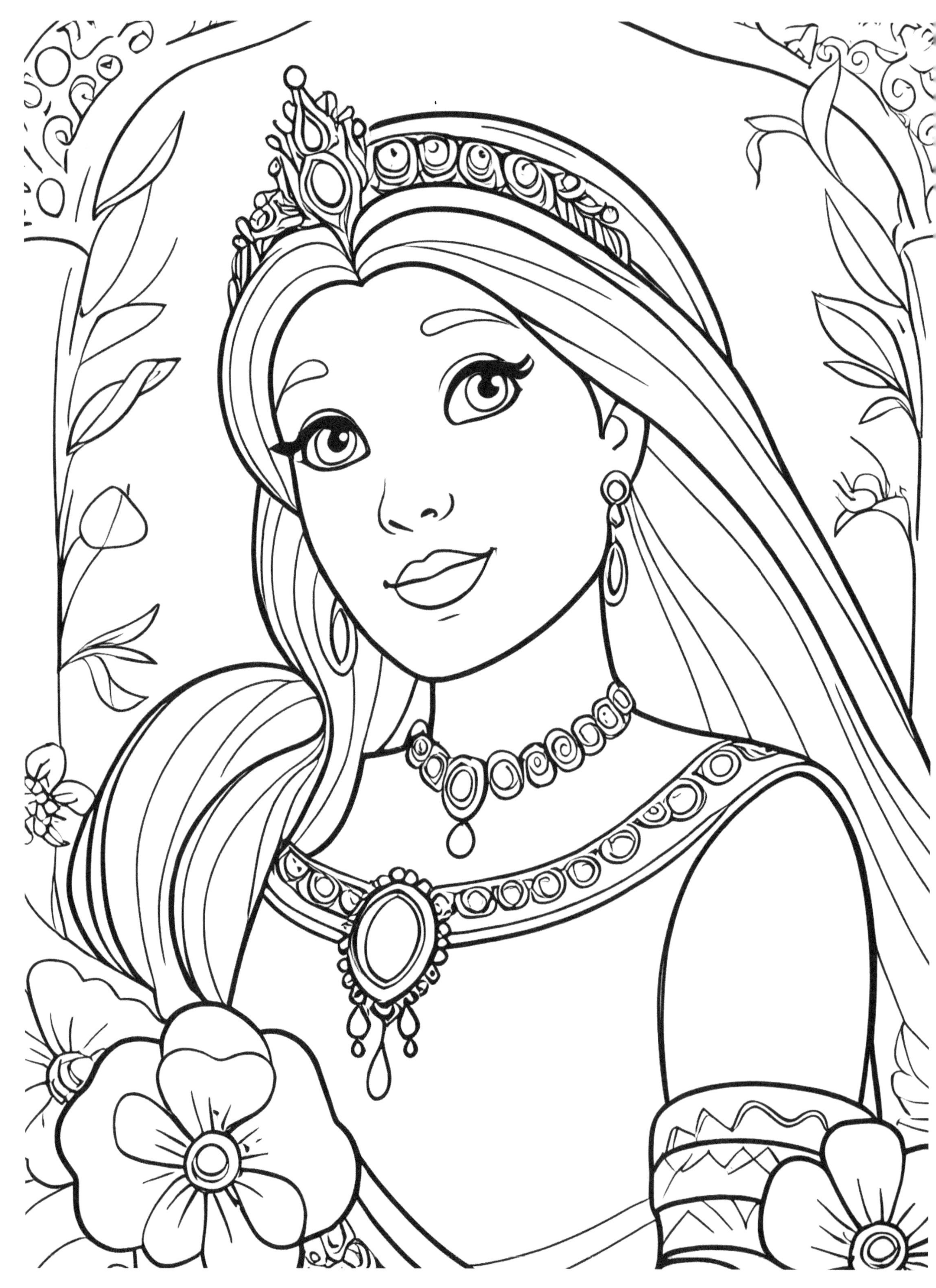

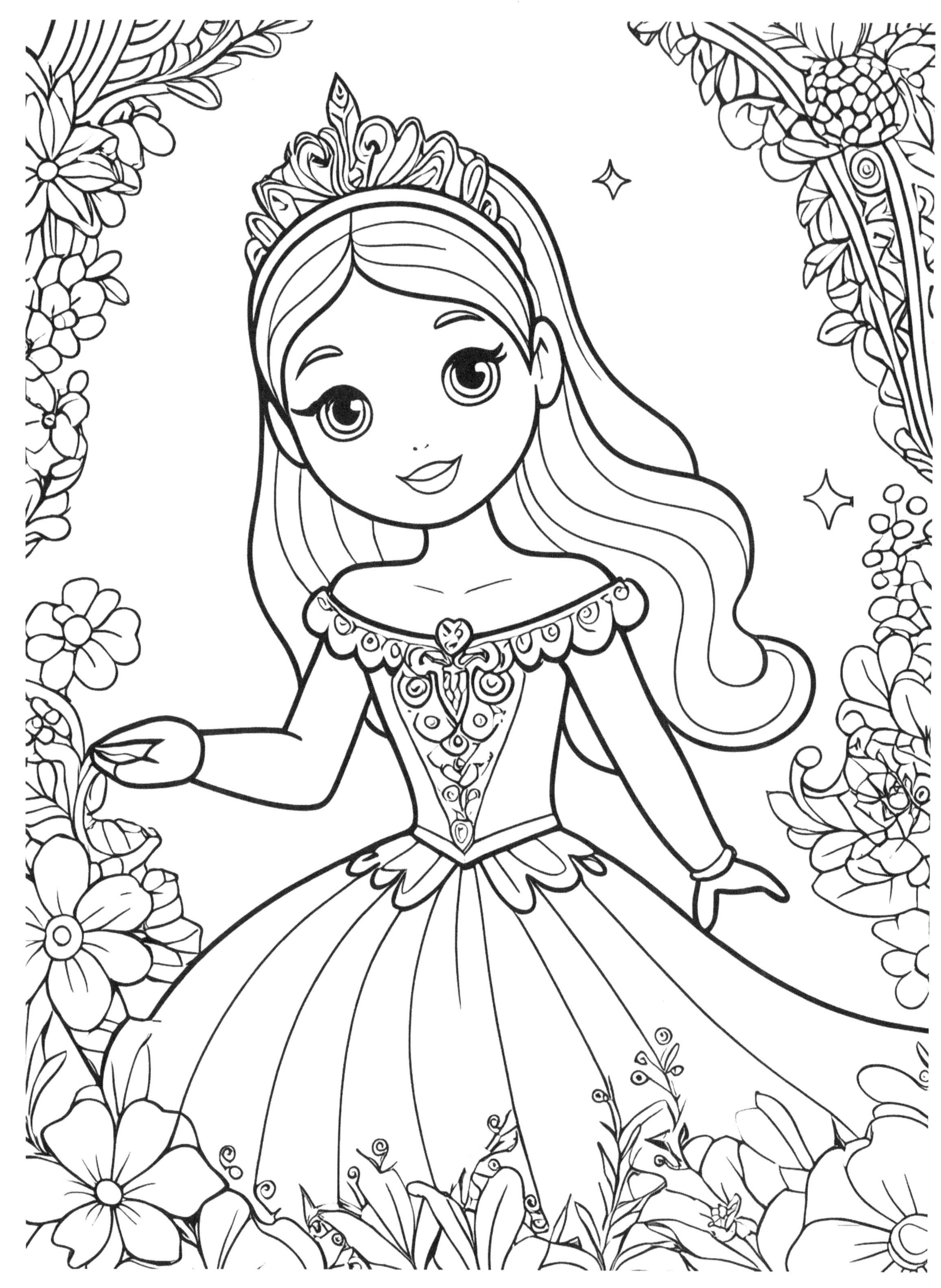

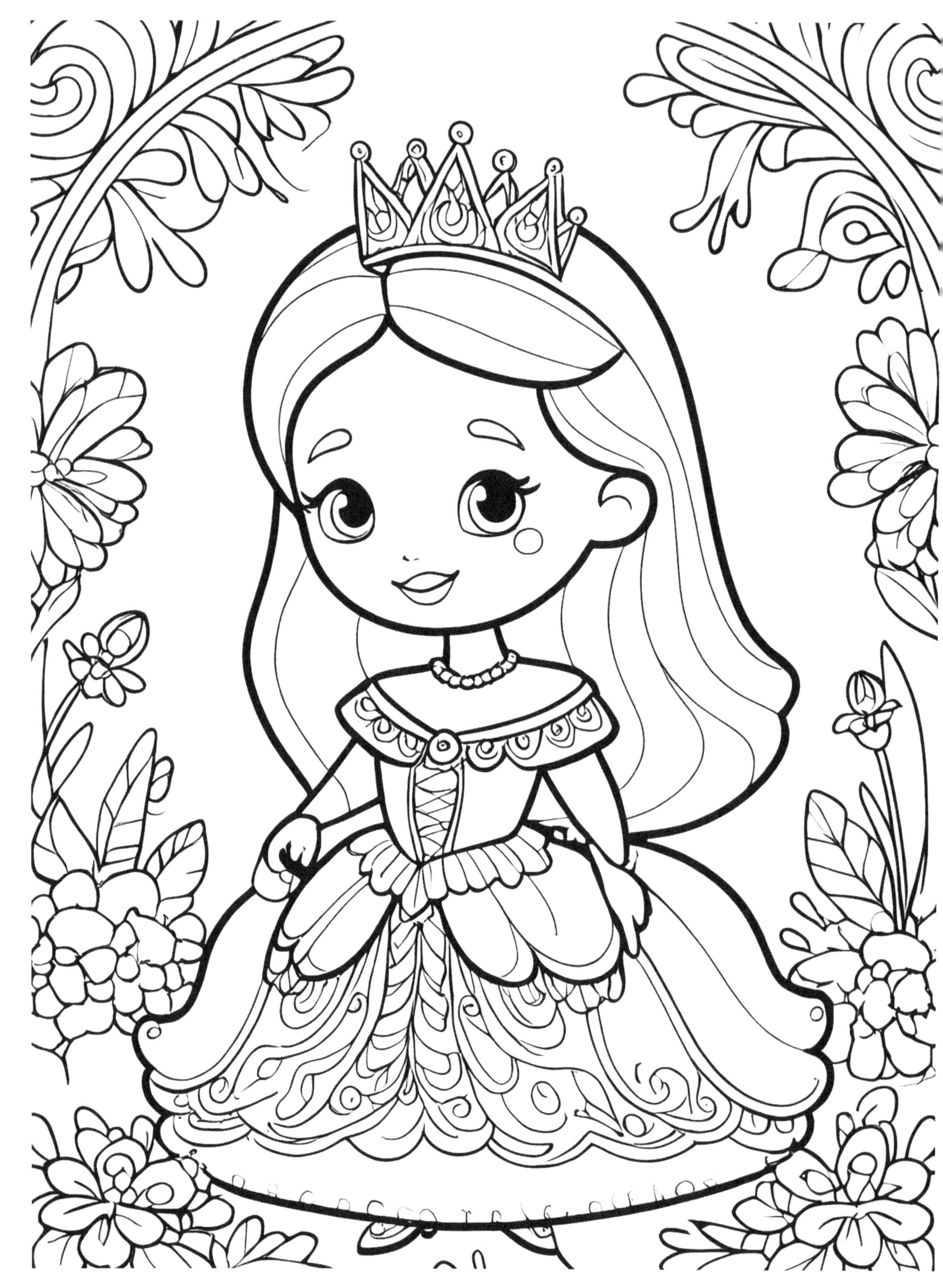

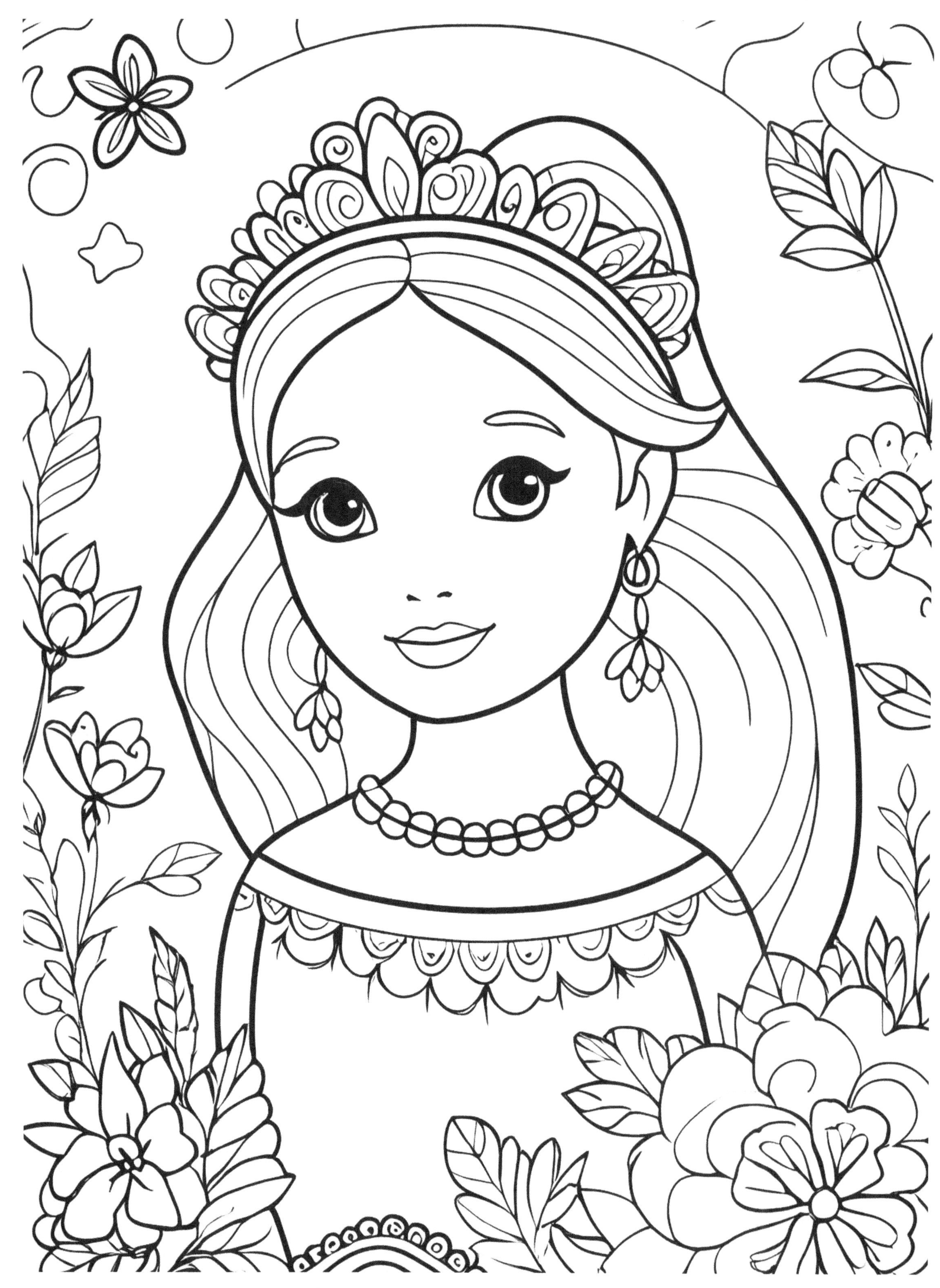

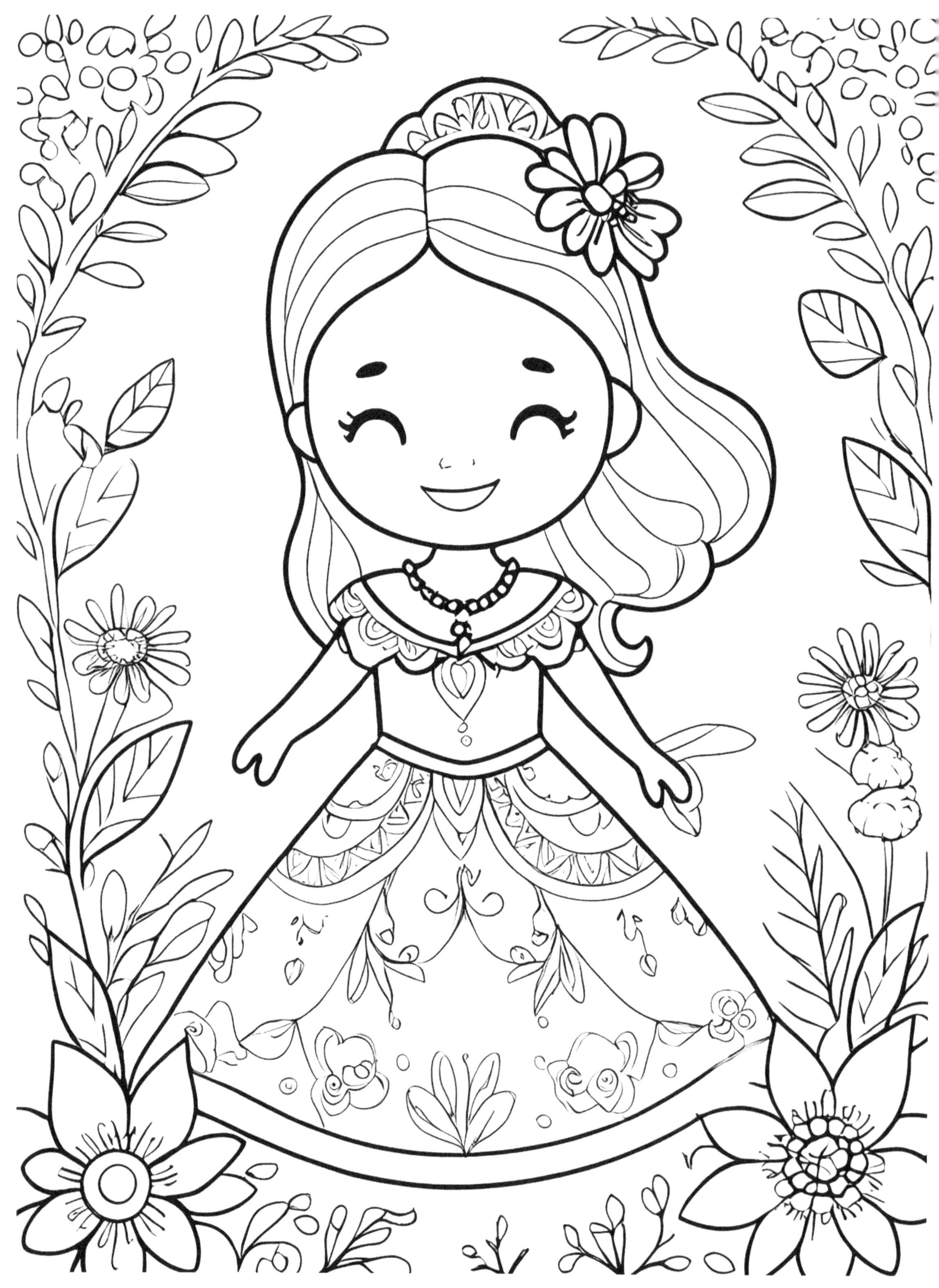

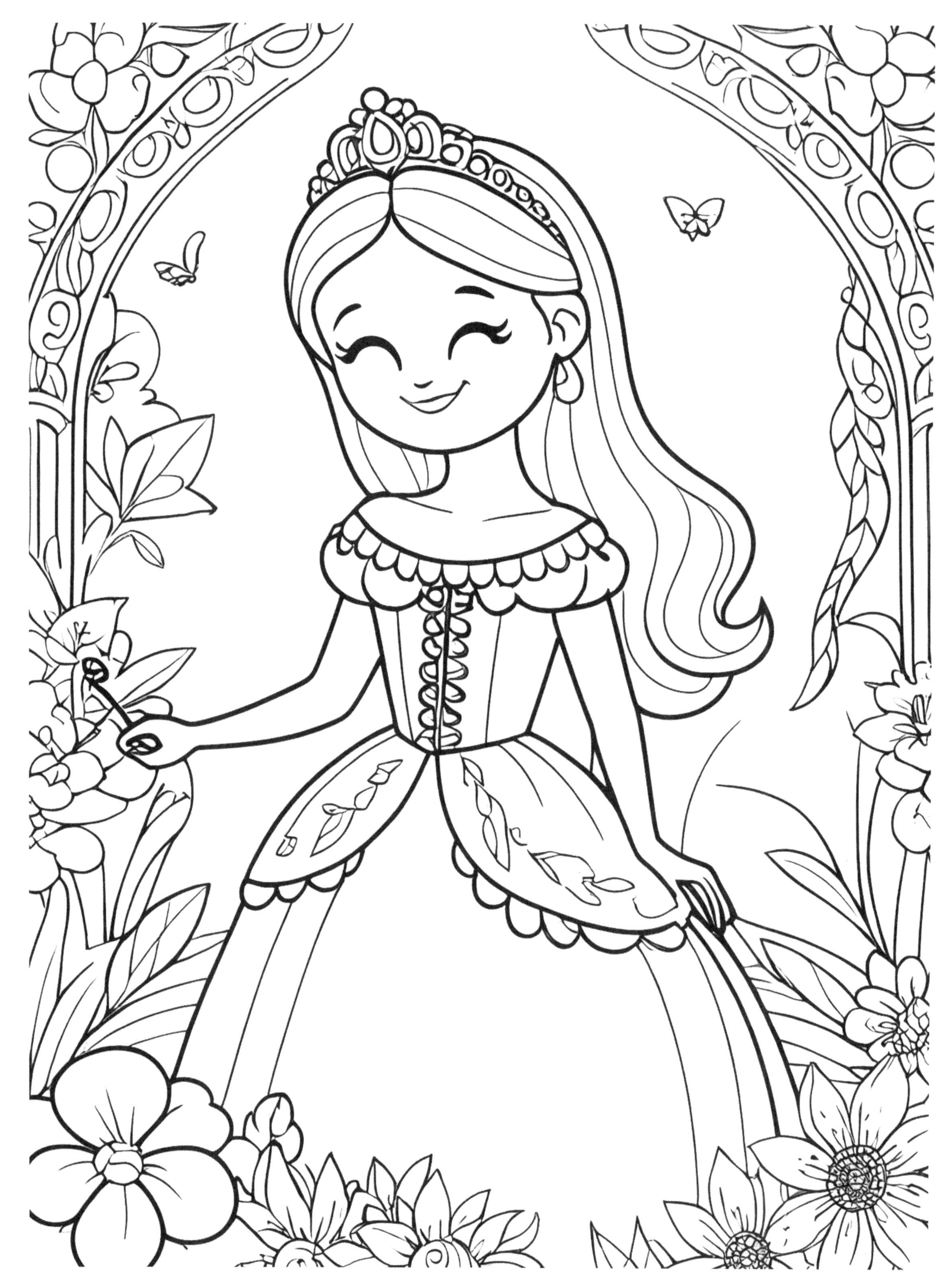

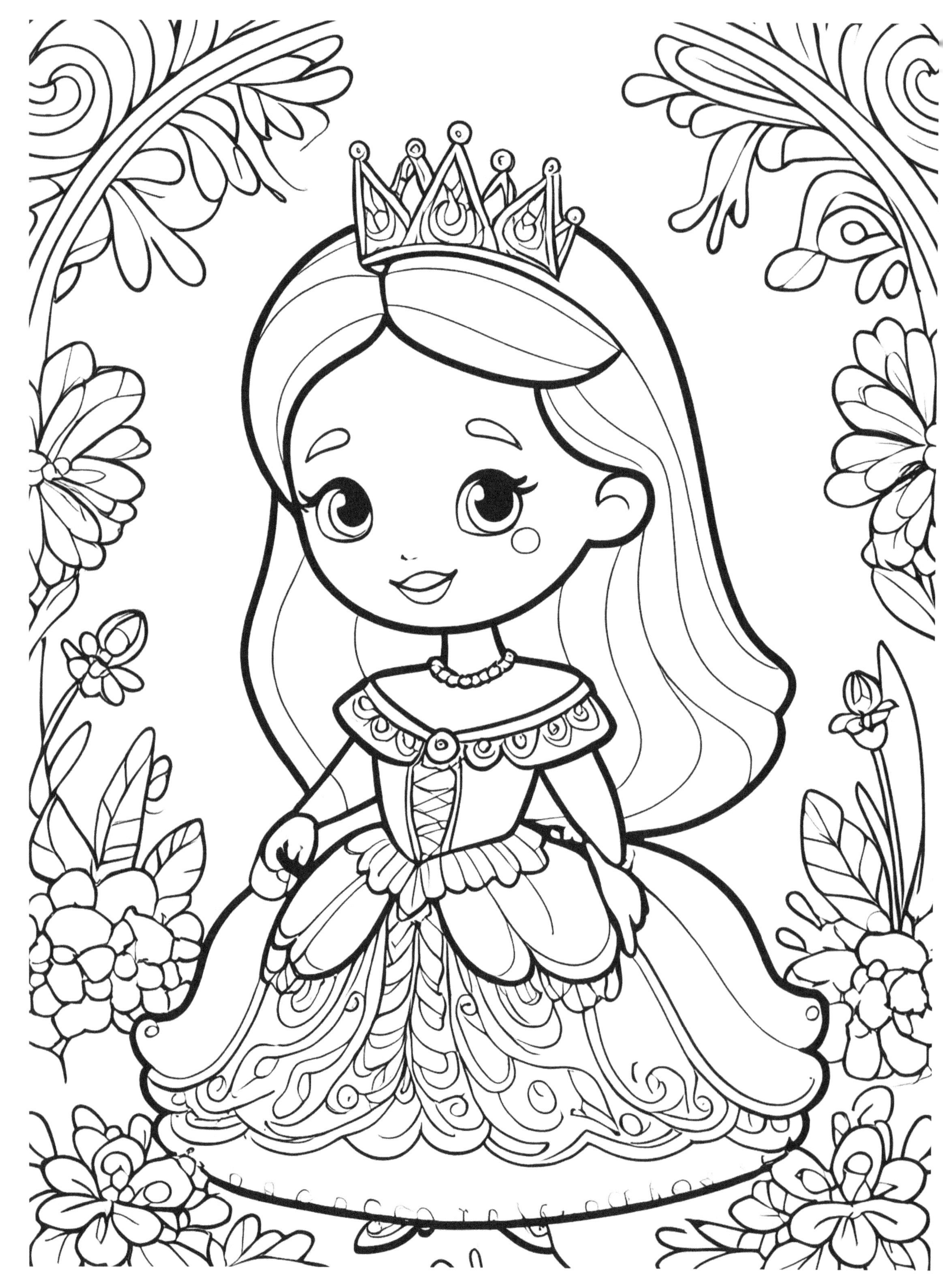

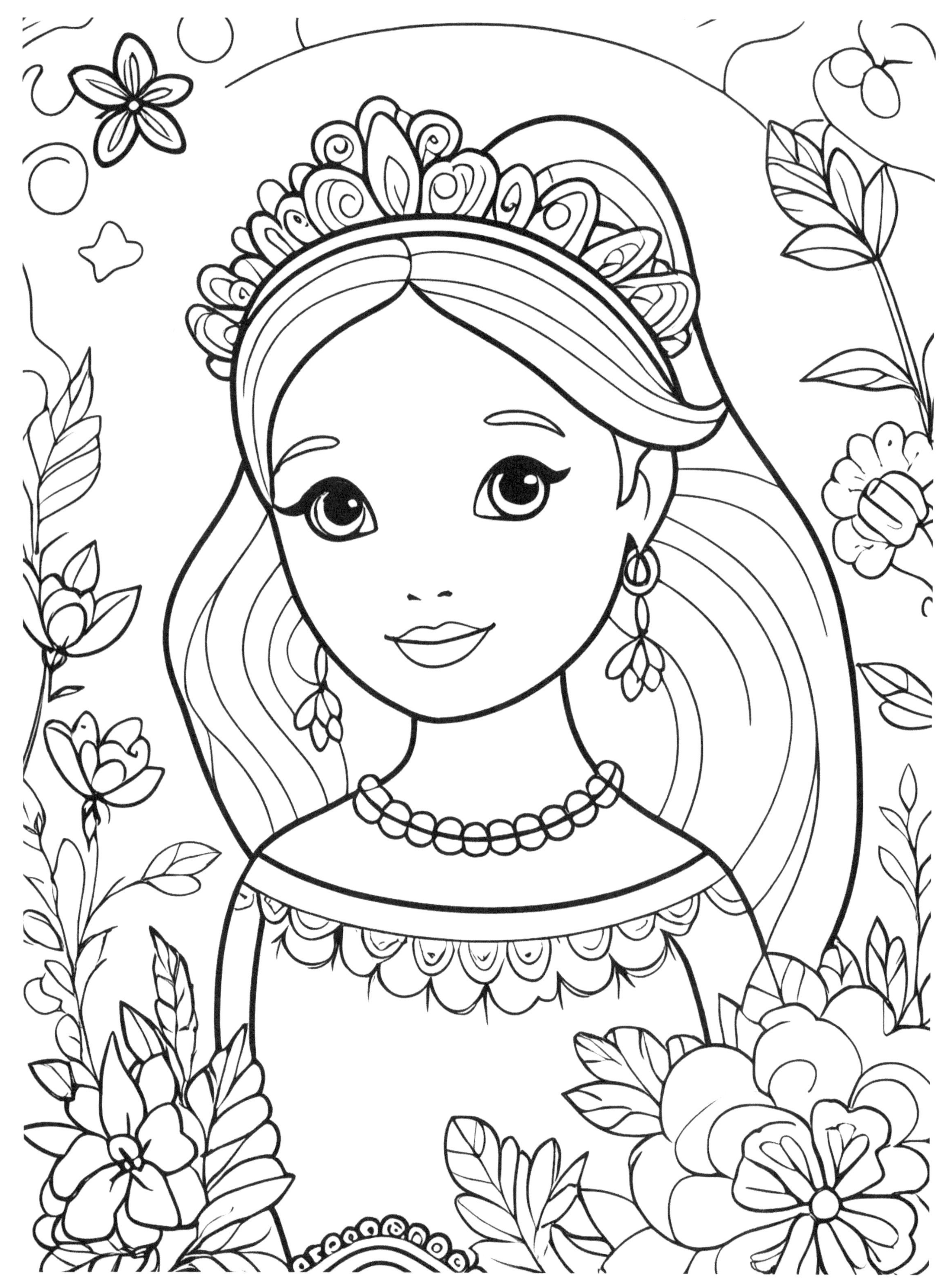

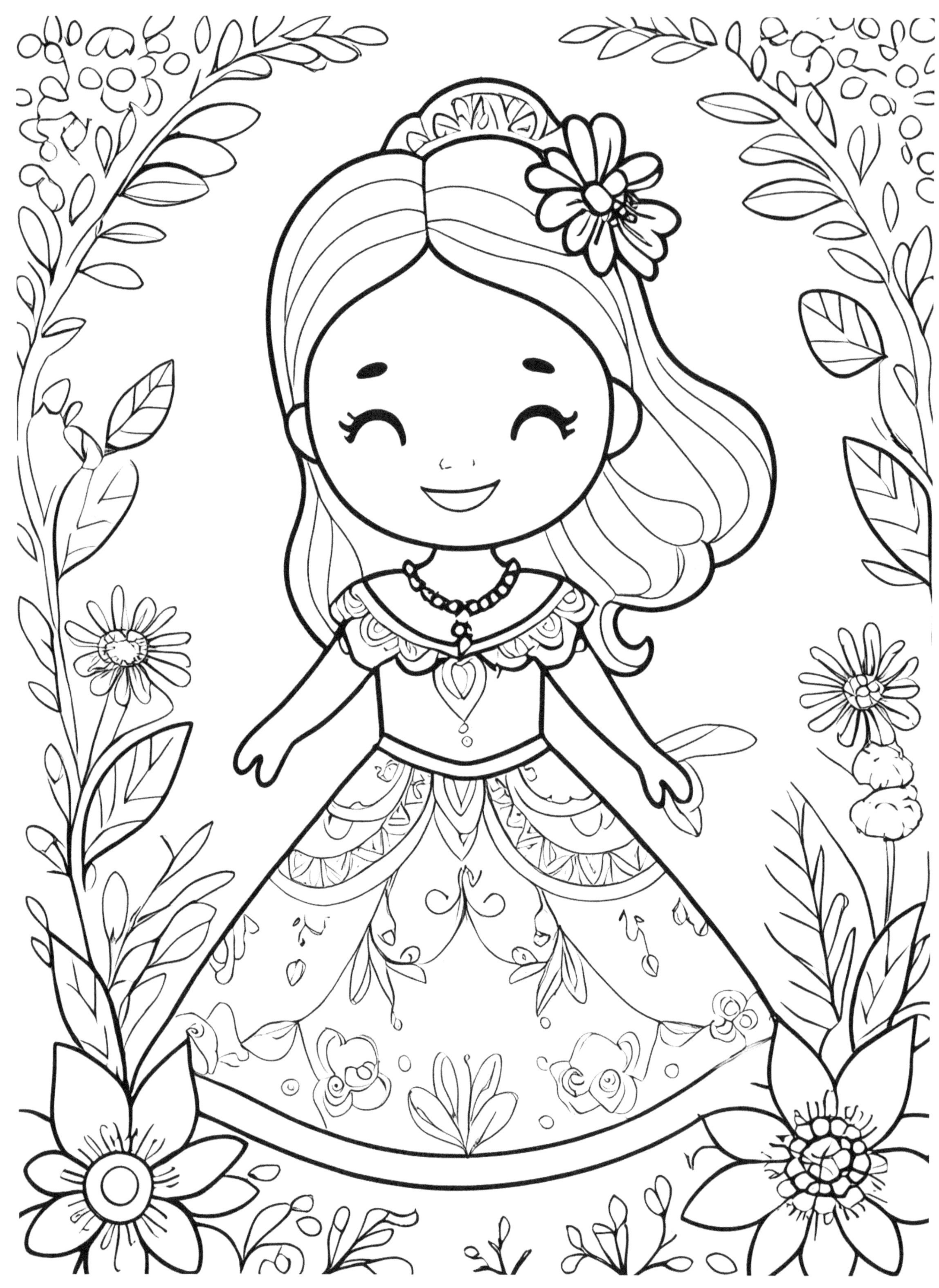

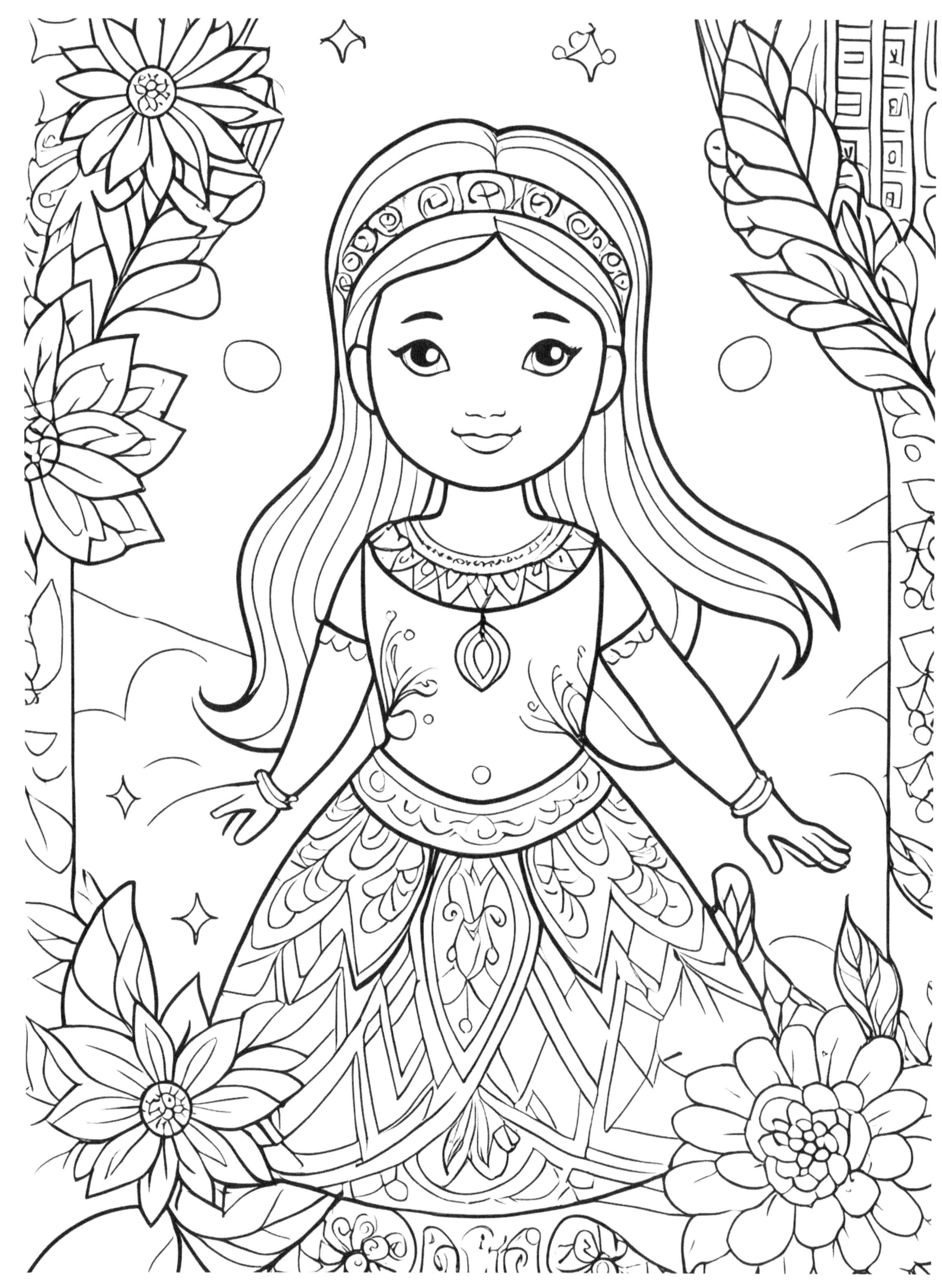

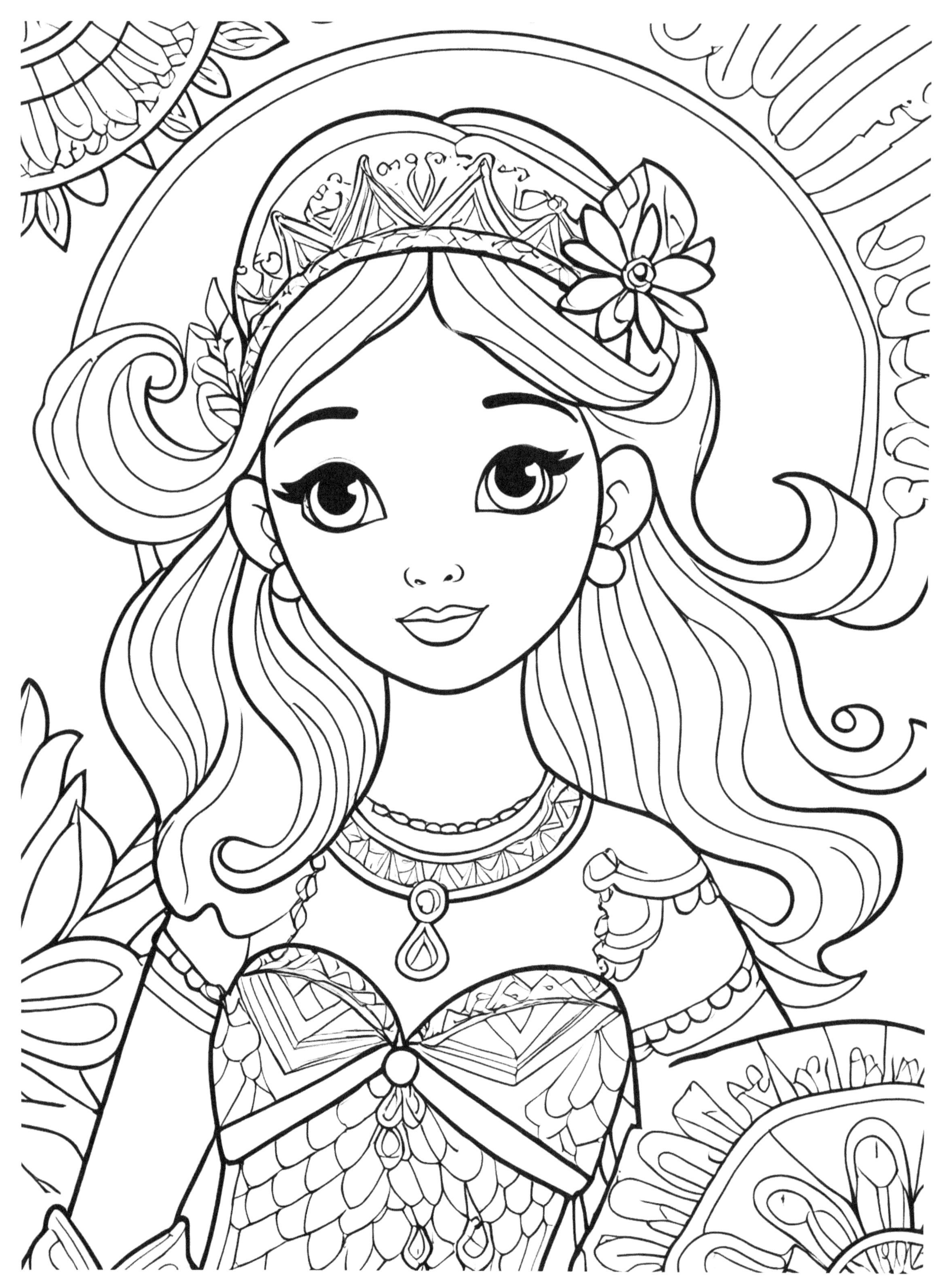

www.ingramcontent.com/pod-product-compliance
Lightning Source LLC
Chambersburg PA
CBHW080034260726
48658CB00007B/2602